J. A. Thompson

London 1970

UNWIN FORUM: 3

THE MONARCHY AND ITS FUTURE

Number One

THE MONARCHY AND ITS FUTURE

ROBERT BLAKE   SASTHI BRATA
JOHN GRIGG   WILLIAM HAMILTON
A. P. HERBERT   GEORGE HIGGINS
CLIVE IRVING   PAUL JOHNSON
GEOFFREY KIRK   HENRY LUCE III
COLIN MACINNES   COMPTON MACKENZIE
DERMOT MORRAH   JEREMY MURRAY-BROWN
CHRISTOPHER OWEN   SIMON RAVEN
NORMAN ST JOHN-STEVAS

with cartoons by

CUMMINGS   DICKENS   GARLAND   GILES   HORNER
JAK   MAHOOD   SCARFE   TROG

Edited by

JEREMY MURRAY-BROWN

London
GEORGE ALLEN AND UNWIN LTD
RUSKIN HOUSE   MUSEUM STREET

FIRST PUBLISHED IN 1969

SBN 04 920024. 0

PRINTED IN GREAT BRITAIN
in 11 *on* 12 *pt Plantin type*
BY WILLMER BROTHERS LIMITED, BIRKENHEAD

PREFACE

This book arose out of a special 'Panorama' programme which I produced for the BBC in November, 1966, on the occasion of Prince Charles's eighteenth birthday, a date of some constitutional significance which gave point to the title: *The Monarchy and Its Future*. As a result of the programme, Peter Leek of Allen and Unwin suggested publishing a collection of essays on the same subject and Philip Unwin then asked me to act as editor.

I was glad to do so as I felt that while television can do certain things excellently and, notably, show how 'popular monarchy' actually strikes ordinary people, the range and depth of its approach are limited. For 'Panorama' we arranged to have a special poll taken to give us a statistical guide to public opinion (*The Listener,* November 17, 1966). This book does not claim to have any such scientific basis. It is only a symposium of individual opinions which broadly cover the spectrum of informed thinking on the subject. It aims to be constructive as well as entertaining.

The names of many of the contributors suggested themselves as belonging to writers who have already made careful studies of the monarchical system. I was anxious to add to these the impressions of outsiders and was delighted at the American and French responses which appear in the book. I also wanted to include at least one essay from someone for whom the monarchy has a real, personal meaning. Rhodesians who rejected UDI suffered a clash of loyalties rarely experienced by British subjects and for them the monarchy suddenly became more than a distant symbol. Christopher Owen describes his own reaction to this tragic dilemma and reminds us that there must be many in Rhodesia who share his feelings. By contrast a young Indian writer draws on a different kind of experience.

Naturally there were refusals which I regretted, though all were courteously phrased. Most came from prominent literary and intellectual figures who did not feel sufficiently roused by the subject. I respect their attitude. 'Once I put the phone down I shan't give it another thought,' said one leading playwright. One of the penalties we pay for having a philistine court is that it is despised by large sections of the intelligentsia. But those who refused would, I think, all agree that a philistine court is preferable to one with highbrow pretensions. Better far a charmed circle of jockeys, punters and yachtsmen, than one of *literati* and eggheads!

I regret also Malcolm Muggeridge's declining to contribute. He wrote, understandably enough, 'The subject bores me to death.' But it was Malcolm Muggeridge who in 1957, with Lord Altrincham, now John Grigg, succeeded in shattering the taboos with which monarchy had become cocooned. In these pages John Grigg now gives his account of the row that broke over their heads that year[1]. At the time Henry Fairlie described in the *Spectator* the kind of letters which Muggeridge and Altrincham had received; they were of a scarcely credible level of filth and offensiveness. The people who wrote them sought a scapegoat for their own hysteria and sense of loss. Muggeridge was their victim; he had lanced the boil and the poison spilled out over himself and his family. I well remember the atmosphere at the BBC at the time. Colleagues were fearful of being called on to stand up and be counted; there were no resignations and few voices were raised in public on his behalf. I should like to record here my feeling of shame at what happened, and my admiration for the fortitude with which he bore it all.

I welcome the opportunity to bring together in this book a series of cartoons by some of our leading artists. Most have been specially drawn for the purpose; Gerald Scarfe's was first published in the *Daily Mirror* in May, 1966 and subsequently shown in 'Panorama'. Giles's appeared originally in the *Daily Express*, and Trog's in the *Observer*. Throughout the first half of this century it would be hard to find a single cartoon in an English publication depicting the reigning British monarch. The tradition of Gillray seemed to have died. I hope this book may prepare for its revival and offer some assistance in pinpointing the right targets.

Jeremy Murray-Brown

[1] The sequence of events was:

(1) *October* 1955: an article by Malcolm Muggeridge in the *New Statesman* entitled 'Royal Soap Opera' caused little stir.

(2) *August* 1957: John Grigg's storm provoking article in the *National and English Review*. (See page 43f.)

(3) *October* 1957: the article by Malcolm Muggeridge in the *Saturday Evening Post* referred to above.

CONTENTS

ROBERT BLAKE

Robert Blake MA, JP, FBA was born in 1916 and educated at King Edward VI School, Norwich, and Magdalen College, Oxford, where he took First Class Honours in Modern Greats in 1938. In the 1939-45 war he served in the Royal Artillery and was in the North African Campaign, 1942. He was a prisoner-of-war from 1942 to 1944, escaped and was mentioned in despatches in 1944. He was a Member (Conservative) of the Oxford City Council from 1957-64. He was Ford's Lecturer in English History for 1967-68, became Student and Tutor in Politics at Christ Church, Oxford in 1947 and was recently appointed Provost of the Queen's College, Oxford.

PUBLICATIONS
The Private Papers of Douglas Haig, 1952; *The Unknown Prime Minister*, 1955; *Disraeli* 1966.

THE CROWN AND POLITICS IN THE TWENTIETH CENTURY

ROBERT BLAKE

'Our Whigs,' wrote Baron Stockmar in 1854 to Prince Albert, 'are nothing but partly conscious, partly unconscious Republicans who stand in the same relation to the throne as the wolf does to the lambs. And these Whigs must have a natural inclination to push to extremity the constitutional fiction . . . that it is unconstitutional to introduce and make use of the name of the irresponsible Sovereign in public debates on matters bearing to the Constitution. But if the English Crown permit a Whig Ministry to follow this rule in practice without exception, you must not wonder if in a little time you find the majority of the people impressed with the belief *that the King in the view of the law is nothing but a mandarin figure which has to nod its head in assent, or shake it in denial, as his Minister pleases.'*

It is the problem of whether or not the monarch is a 'mandarin figure' which this chapter attempts to answer. Has the view attributed by Stockmar to the Whigs prevailed, or does some residue of political power still attach to the British monarchy?

The question is not easy to answer. The prestige of the crown is still very great. Gone are the days of a serious republican movement, like that of Dilke and Chamberlain in the early 1870s. Even on the Left the tradition of Keir Hardie has long ago vanished, and it is unlikely that Mr Wilson will make the abolition of the monarchy his programme at the next election. True, till recently there was one curious corner where the republican fire still burned with however erratic and flickering a flame. But Lord Beaverbrook, whose personal dislike of the crown was notorious and emerged from time to time in some of his papers, is no longer with us. For many years past even jokes about royalty have been perilous. One can scarcely imagine the sort of anti-royal cartoons in which Sir Max Beerbohm excelled being published today.

Prestige and respect are not the same as power, and power is not the same as influence. There is undoubtedly widespread public ignorance about the monarch's power. A private survey conducted in 1966 (not published) confirmed what casual inquiry suggests. Asked the question which would prevail if the opinions of the Queen and the Prime Minister conflicted, a substantial majority of the sample interrogated thought that the Queen's would. What is more they not only believed that hers *would* prevail, they also believed that it *should*. This latter opinion, and, given the public's capacity for wishful thinking, perhaps the former too, may reflect the general scepticism about politicians which seems to have been gathering momentum in the 1960s. But whatever the explanation, it is a view of monarchical power that runs clean contrary to the lessons of even the most elementary books on modern history and on modern constitutional usage. It raises incidentally the intriguing problem of what would have happened if King Edward VIII had defied the leaders of all three political parties and forced a general election on the question of his marriage to Mrs Simpson.

No doubt the constitutional position of the monarchy is one of those matters in which the gap between well-informed educated opinion and unsophisticated popular belief is at its widest. Yet those who regard themselves as well-informed would be wrong to be too superior or condescending. The British Constitution with its absence of clear legal rules and its ever changing penumbra of custom, usage and convention does not lend itself easily to precise exposition at any single moment of time. And of all its component parts the monarchy is the least easy to define and to analyse.

The British Royal Family is the oldest reigning house in Europe. The Queen is lineally descended from William the Conqueror. Although there have been disputed successions, *coups d'état* and civil wars, the institution of hereditary monarchy has had a continuous existence, in however many changing shapes, from the conquest to the present day, except for a short gap of eleven years between the judicial murder of Charles I in 1649 and the restoration of his elder son in 1660. For the first two and a half centuries of this immense period the monarchy was absolute in the sense that no set of laws or customs limited its operation. That is not to say that the king could do precisely what he pleased. On the contrary the most despotic of the Norman rulers found it prudent to introduce into their governance some element of consent at least among the great feudal and clerical dignitaries. But the balance varied from monarch to monarch, and the boundaries of royal power remained fluid and ill-defined.

The first step towards a definition was Magna Carta in 1215. Its exact significance has been the subject of much historical dispute, but no one denies that it marked a change of lasting importance. For it was in effect a bargain or treaty between the king and the 'common council of our realm' whose consent was now required for certain taxes, and it contained a series of guarantees and reforms which could never be wholly disregarded henceforth. It marked a first stage in the prolonged transition from royal absolutism to a 'limited monarchy'. As F. W. Maitland, the greatest of all constitutional historians, puts it, 'In form the Charter is a Charter, a free grant by the king, in reality a code of reforming laws passed by the whole body of bishops and barons and thrust upon a reluctant king.'

The 'common council' to which the Charter referred was a feudal assembly of archbishops, bishops, abbots, greater and lesser barons (the distinction between these latter is a matter of controversy which need not detain us). Eighty years later the institution known as parliament had come into being. Its great distinguishing feature was that it contained, in addition to the feudal magnates of the common council, representatives of the counties and of the cities and boroughs. For a time the common council and parliament existed side by side and no clear demarcation seems to have been made between the sort of measures that each could enact. But the important point had become established that the king could not make laws without the consent of one of them, and in due course 'the king in parliament' became the sole authority for taxation and the enactment of statutes. Of course statutes were not the only form of legislation and a prolonged dispute rumbled on about the king's power to make 'ordinances' and other decrees – a lesser form of law-making but one which if pushed too far would destroy the whole authority of parliament. The dispute was not finally settled in favour of parliament until the deposition of James II and the accession of William III.

Long before that, parliament had become so deeply rooted in the constitutional soil of England that its suppression or removal was exceedingly difficult. After the days of the Norman and

Angevin kings there was only one period when effective royal absolutism prevailed – the reigns of Henry VII and Henry VIII and perhaps the later Tudors too. Yet it is significant that they ruled through and not against parliament. It was a subservient, packed parliament, no doubt, but there was no question of its being bypassed or abolished. It thus suited the Tudors to elevate the status of parliament in order to bolster up their own despotism. But this very abuse of its powers by the Tudor kings was to be a valuable precedent for parliament when in the next century it sought to assert its rights against the Stuarts. The intricacies of that great social, legal, constitutional, and military struggle, the English Revolution, cannot be described here. It is enough to say that by the end the English monarchy, almost alone among all its European counterparts, was a 'limited monarchy' in which the king, though he still ruled as well as reigned, was subject to restrictions and limitations unparalleled elsewhere.

The Hanoverian monarchies of the eighteenth and early nineteenth centuries still possessed real power. The king was the head of the executive with the right to appoint to a multitude of posts from the great offices of state downwards. There was, however, no question of his by-passing parliament whose complete control over taxation and legislation had been established beyond dispute. George III, so often represented in old-fashioned history books as aiming at despotic power, never dreamed of being anything but a constitutional monarch. Indeed if he had been more ready to disregard parliament or to play if off against the various colonial legislatures in North America he might not have lost the American colonies. If we are to seek any modern parallel to the Hanoverian monarchy it is the American presidency. The founding fathers set up what was in effect an elective monarchy but one purged of the great defects which, as they saw it, made the actual monarchy in England odious and tyrannical. And of all these defects reformers regarded the worst as being the king's influence over parliament. Hence the separation of the executive from the legislative power, which is such an important feature of the American Constitution.

No such separation existed in Britain. The key to the king's position lay in the fact that crown patronage, exercised by the First Lord of the Treasury and other ministers whom he appointed, normally ensured a parliamentary majority for the king's appointees. This would have been impossible if the holders of offices of profit under the crown had, as radical opinion demanded, been entirely excluded from the House of Commons, or if the great majority of parliamentary constituencies had not been wide open to jobbery, corruption and 'influence', to use the euphemistic contemporary expression. As it was, the system ensured not only that the king's ministers would win any general election in normal circumstances, but that they would, again in normal circumstances, retain their majority in the House between elections, provided that – and here lay the real power of the king – they also retained the confidence of the king whose right to dismiss them without notice or reason given was never disputed. The king had to find ministers who could manage parliament, and to that extent his freedom of choice was limited, but the mere fact of being the king's ministers gave his appointees an almost, though not quite, unchallengeable position in parliament. Between 1715 and 1835 no government lost a general election.

The next big change occurred as a result of two concurrent movements, the campaign to cut down crown patronage in the interest of what was called 'economical reform' and the campaign to put the parliamentary franchise on a rational basis – a campign in which the first great victory was won with the Reform Act of 1832. The result was soon seen. In 1834 William IV dismissed Lord Melbourne and appointed Sir Robert Peel in his place as Prime Minister. On past form Peel ought to have had no difficulty in winning the ensuing general election. In the event, although he improved his parliamentary position, the Conservatives were defeated and the King had to take Melbourne back again. The King was furious and declared that he would not ask the Whig ministers to dinner. They carried on undeterred by this threat. Since that day no monarch has dismissed a prime minister. The crown's prestige could not survive many such defeats, and with the loss of the power of its ministers to 'make' a parliamentary majority, there could no longer be any guarantee of success. The alternative to a series of political conflicts which were bound in the end to damage the crown irretrievably was withdrawal into political neutrality. This is in fact what happened and the long reign of Queen Victoria saw the transformation of the monarchy from an active force in politics into the impartial pivot upon which the Constitution hinges.

The process was eased by the well-established constitutional doctrine that the king or queen normally took no action except upon the advice of a minister who was constitutionally 'responsible' for it to parliament and who alone could be called to account. As long as the monarch was able to choose his ministers and guarantee their parliamentary majority, he could within limits get the advice he wanted and ensure that, even if it was bitterly criticized, it would at least be upheld in parliament. But the diminution in his effective choice of ministers involved a corresponding diminution in his effective control over policy and patronage. The change meant a decisive shift of power first to parliament – particularly the lower house – and ultimately, with the democratization of the franchise, to the electorate itself.

This is not to say that Queen Victoria had no freedom at all in her choice of prime minister. During the first thirty years of her reign the House of Commons was often in a state of political fluidity, with no party or group in possession of a clear majority. In such circumstances there might be more than one combination of the political pack capable of winning the game. In 1852 the Queen might have appointed somebody other than Lord Aberdeen. In 1859 it was not inevitable that she should choose Palmerston. Russell was equally possible. But that particular crisis also showed the limitations on her power of choice. As a means of avoiding either of 'those two dreadful old men' as she called them, she tried to impose Lord Granville, but failed because Palmerston and Russell, though each was willing to serve under the other, were not prepared to serve under Granville and he was not prepared to form a government without them.

This limited freedom of choice became further limited with constitutional developments in the latter half of her reign. From 1868 onwards general elections began to produce clear verdicts in favour of one or other of the two big parties. In such circumstances the Queen was bound to choose the acknowledged leader of the majority party, however much she disliked him. In 1886 she privately described Gladstone as 'this half crazy and in many ways ridiculous old man', and in 1892 as 'that dangerous old fanatic', but on both occasions she had to accept him as prime minister. The Liberals had a majority and no other Liberal would have attempted to form a government unless Gladstone had been asked first and had refused.

There remained, however, one situation in which the monarch might have a real element of choice. What would happen if there was no acknowledged party leader? This could occur in those days in one of two eventualities. First a party might come into office with its leadership divided or 'in commission' between the leader in the House of Lords and the leader in the Commons. Nineteenth-century political parties had no machinery for electing a leader of the party as a whole. True, anyone who had once been prime minister and who had not declared an intent to step down possessed a sort of understood primacy. But there could be occasions when no such figure existed. Thus in 1885 when Gladstone was defeated in the House and resigned the Queen had a limited but real choice among the opposition leaders. Disraeli had died four years earlier. There was no living Tory ex-prime minister. Lord Salisbury had been elected leader of the Tory peers, Sir Stafford Northcote of the Tory MPs. The Queen chose Lord Salisbury. She was quite right on all personal grounds. Salisbury was younger, abler, and in far better health. But no one at the time could have argued that it would be unconstitutional to choose Northcote. The possibility of this kind of option gradually faded away. It was hard to say precisely when a peer prime minister was no longer a runner. In 1923 Lord Curzon and in 1940 Lord Halifax were seriously regarded as such, though in the event the one was nobbled and the other declined to come under starters' orders. At all events it is not a possibility today.

The second eventuality in which royal choice could matter was where a prime minister with a majority in the House behind him either died or resigned without leaving any single obvious successor. The question whether the monarch still has any independent power or has become simply the mandarin figure feared by Baron Stockmar largely turns on a consideration of this case, and therefore one must look at past precedents with some care.

The reason why the monarch's invitation to form a government differs from all his other acts is clear enough. By definition it cannot be done on ministerial 'advice' in the constitutional sense of the word because no minister is there to 'advise'. The resigning prime minister cannot take constitutional responsibility for an act which he will not be present to defend, and clearly no one else can do so. The argument that the new prime minister takes retrospective responsibility for his own appointment strains common sense, and the better view would seem to be that in this case ministerial responsibility does not apply. Of course this does not necessarily mean that a real choice exists. In many, perhaps most, cases there is an obvious successor to the retiring prime minister. Balfour, Asquith, Neville Chamberlain, Anthony Eden were regarded as the inevitable heirs to Salisbury, Campbell-Bannerman, Baldwin and Churchill. In each case any other choice would have caused great surprise and grave criticism.

Nevertheless, there have been four instances during the last three-quarters of a century where the choice was not obvious in the sense that informed opinion regarded it beforehand as a foregone conclusion. The first occurred in 1894 when Gladstone, aged, ailing and frustrated, at last resigned. The parliamentary party if consulted would probably have plumped for Sir William Harcourt, the Chancellor of the Exchequer. The Cabinet if consulted would have preferred Lord Rosebery, the Foreign Secretary. Gladstone, if consulted, would have advised in favour of Lord Spencer, the First Lord of the Admiralty. The Queen consulted no one, and chose Rosebery whose political stance was more congenial to her than that of the others and whom she liked personally. Rosebery was a disastrous prime minister but it is by no means clear that his rivals would have fared better.

The next occasion was in 1923 when Bonar Law who had won a comfortable electoral victory seven months earlier was obliged to resign through ill health. The obvious contenders for his place were Stanley Baldwin, who, though Chancellor of the Exchequer, was relatively unknown at the time, and George Nathaniel, the Marquess Curzon of Kedleston who was Foreign Secretary – a famous figure cast in the mould and manner of the eighteenth century, very rich, thanks to a fortune inherited from his American first wife, Grace Leiter, far more distingushed in the public service than any rival but somehow faintly comic and slightly anachronistic. The King unlike Queen Victoria was anxious to ascertain the views of the outgoing Prime Minister, but Bonar Law felt too ill to be consulted. The King's Private Secretary made enquiries among highly placed members of the Conservative Party. He received conflicting opinions, but the one that carried most weight was Balfour's. The Tory elder statesman had never thought much of Curzon but he based the case for

Baldwin exclusively upon the importance of the prime minister being in the House of Commons. When he returned from London to the house party where he had been staying in Norfolk, one of the ladies, so the story goes, said to him, 'Will dear George get it?' 'No, dear George will not.' 'He will be terribly disappointed.' 'I don't know. Even if he has lost the hope of glory he still possesses the means of grace.' Curzon bore his defeat with courage and magnanimity although on the news being broken he stigmatized Baldwin as a man of the utmost mediocrity. Nevertheless there can be little doubt that the decision was right both on party and national grounds. Baldwin was a better prime minister than Curzon could ever have been.

In 1957 an even more difficult choice arose, for this time no argument about the House of Lords could be brought into the scales. Anthony Eden was advised early in January that his health was too uncertain for him to continue. The Queen had to choose as his successor either Mr R. A. Butler or Mr Harold Macmillan. The general public (i.e. most journalists) expected Mr Butler to be the choice. In the event it was Mr Macmillan. Many accounts have been given of the way in which the decision was reached. It would be wrong to rely too much on any of them. But it seems clear that, to an even greater extent than in 1923, and quite unlike 1894, an effort was made to discover the Conservative party's opinion. There is every reason to believe, contrary to many allegations, that Sir Anthony Eden was consulted, though a proper discretion has concealed the nature of his advice. It seems to be generally agreed that the opinions of the Cabinet and of leading back benchers were canvassed, also those of prominent figures in the party organization. Only one person has actually told us what his advice was. Sir Winston, an exception to all rules, not only called at Buckingham Palace on the crucial day but two years later announced to his constituency executive that he had advised in favour of Mr Macmillan. 'I was delighted,' he said, 'that my recommendation was acted on.' The historian should, however, be wary of assuming that it settled the matter. It is worth noticing that the Labour party took the opportunity to announce that in analogous circumstances it would not leave the matter to the crown. No Labour minister would accept the premiership till he had first been elected leader of the parliamentary party.

The fourth occasion for royal choice in this kind of situation may well turn out to have been the last. This was Sir Alec Douglas-Home's appointment in 1963. Once again an unexpected resignation, this time at a singularly inopportune moment, the start of the annual Conservative Conference at Blackpool and the nadir of the party's popularity, left no obvious heir apparent. Indeed whereas in the previous cases the field had at least been limited to two, in this case a host of contenders threw their hats into the ring. The issue was complicated by the Peerage Renunciation Bill which made it possible for members of the House of Lords to put themselves in the running; and the busy hum of intrigue was punctuated from time to time by the tinkle of falling coronets. From his sick bed Mr Macmillan co-ordinated the various enquiries made by the Whips and others about party sentiment. The upshot was that he advised the Queen to send for the Earl of Home, and Mr Butler, his chief rival, was passed over for the second time.

The episode caused violent controversy in the Conservative party. The supporters of Mr Butler, furious at defeat, professed to see in it the occult working of a 'magic circle' of old Etonian aristocrats determined to keep the premiership in their hands. This was nonsense. There is not the smallest reason to suppose that Sir Alec Home would not have been chosen on a free vote among Conservative MPs. The fact remained that no such vote had been openly taken, and so the matter could never be proved, however elaborate the informal consultations had been. It was clear that a repetition of this sort of 'emergence' of a prime minister, and hence of a party leader, would come under increasing fire in future.

Sir Alec Home, by now leader of the opposition, took the initiative early in 1965 and announced a machinery for the future election of the party leader. Its details are rather more complicated than the procedure laid down in the Labour Party's standing orders, but the principle is the same, election by the parliamentary party; and it is clear that the process will apply whether the party is in power or in opposition. In July, 1965 Mr Heath was elected as leader under the new disposition.

In form, then, the crown would seem to have lost its last residue of effective power. The two main parties appear to be agreed, if on nothing else, that no one should accept the office of prime minister unless he has been first elected leader of the party. This seems to mean that the crown's choice is *de facto* limited to one person. Labour has held this opinion for many years, but it so happens that there has never been a change of leadership when they were in office, and the matter has not yet been put to the test. The Conservatives from 1911 to 1965 were in the opposite position. Their changes had always occurred when they were in office; they had been content to allow a new prime minister to 'emerge' through the traditional method of royal choice, and for his leadership of the party to be ratified formally afterwards.[1] No doubt the 'choice' of the monarch ever since 1894 has been approximating more and more to an informal sounding of party opinion and a search for a concensus, and it has been moving further and further away from Queen Victoria's notion of choosing the man whom she considered the 'best' prime minister. Although under a party system the two concepts overlap, for the ablest statesman will get nowhere if he does not command the support of his party, there is a difference between them nonetheless. The crown under the old order, in fact if not in form, chose the party's leader. The party under the new order will, in fact if not in form, be choosing the crown's first minister.

Is this, then, the end of a long road? Has the monarch finally and irrevocably become 'nothing but a mandarin figure' nodding his head, either as 'his Minister' pleases or, in the case of appointment of that minister, as the majority party pleases? We are not concerned here with Bagehot's 'three rights – the right to be consulted, the right to encourage, the right to warn'. These are of the greatest importance in any assessment of the monarchy, and the longer the monarch's experience, the more important they become. But they are examples of influence, not power. Can influence exist for long, if there is no longer any power at all behind it, not even, to lift from its context a famous phrase of Lord Salisbury 'the shadow of the shred after the rag itself has been torn away'?

Without answering the last question one can, I think, safely assert that the British monarch, in spite of all the changes out-

---

[1] The exception was Bonar Law in October 1922 who refused formally to 'kiss hands' until he had been elected leader of the party in place of Austen Chamberlain.

lined earlier, has not become a mere mandarin figure. Rightly in an age of popular democracy the crown does not intervene in the normal working of the political system. In retrospect one can see the situations of 1957 and 1963 as anachronistic. The Conservative party ought to have devised an elective system for choosing its leader in such circumstances much earlier. The promulgation of the present procedure in 1965 was long overdue, and it should relieve the crown of an embarrassing burden. But this does not mean that the crown's responsibility has in all circumstances been shifted to the majority of the majority party. In normal circumstances, no doubt it has, but circumstances are not always normal.

There have been three instances in this century where prime ministers have taken office, although they were not, and in two cases had no prospect of being elected as leaders of their parties: Lloyd George in 1916; Ramsay MacDonald in 1931; Winston Churchill in 1940. The common feature of all three episodes was a national crisis in which the king played the role of mediator. It is difficult to see how the result could have been achieved if election to party leadership had been a pre-requisite. The Liberals would not have elected Lloyd George in a contest with Asquith. Ramsay MacDonald was actually expelled from the Labour party after forming the National Government in 1931. Churchill's reception from the Conservative benches when he first took office in 1940 was anything but cordial, and Neville Chamberlain retained the party leadership. True, Churchill had no trouble in getting himself elected a few months later when Chamberlain was forced to retire through ill health, but much had happened in the interval. No doubt such crises have been and will be rare. No doubt the emergence of the particular person as prime minister in each case was made possible by the inability or unwillingness of the party leaders to press their claims. But the fact remains that the monarch's role was important and discretionary, and that the result could not have been achieved by the mechanical application of automatic rules.

To put it another way, circumstances may still arise in which more than one politician can command a parliamentary majority. This situation was a regular feature of mid-Victorian politics and it gave the Queen a certain latitude of choice. It has become highly exceptional now, because of the increased rigidity of parties, the normal conclusiveness of general elections, and the rules about leadership which all the parties have adopted. But the exceptional can sometimes happen, and it is still possible to envisage circumstances of national emergency in which the monarch's role in the formation of some sort of coalition government would not be simply that of a rubber stamp.

So much then for the one power which, it is agreed, the monarch can exert, indeed must exert, without following ministerial 'advice' in the technical sense of the word. What of the possibility of the monarch refusing to accept such advice in cases where it is normally regarded as binding? Has the crown any discretion at all in this field? Clearly not, in 999 cases out of a thousand, for the reasons already given. The prime minister and his government would resign, and, even if alternative advisers could be found and even if they were supported in parliament perhaps after a general election, the crown would have been pulled into politics and would be in danger of becoming, as Asquith put it in a famous memorandum to King George V, 'the football of the contending factions'. The monarch must be consulted and is entitled to warn, but in normal circumstances this is the limit to which he can go.

There is, however, one prerogative which though not quite analogous to the choice of a prime minister has a slightly different status from others exercised on ministerial advice. This is the question of the dissolution of parliament. No one, I think, would now seriously argue that the monarch could force a dissolution against the will of the prime minister – except perhaps in the extreme case of a government which without the excuse of an emergency attempted against the will of the opposition to prolong itself in power by repealing the Quinquennial Act. But it is not so clear that the monarch could never refuse a dissolution requested by a prime minister. George V regarded himself as having the right to do so, though he never in fact exercised it, and no one has seriously disputed his claim.

The most recent occasion when the point arose was in 1950. Mr Attlee had just won an election by only six seats. It seemed possible that he might be defeated in the House and ask for a second dissolution almost at once; and a lengthy correspondence followed in *The Times* in which some eminent constitutionalists argued that the King should refuse. Sir John Wheeler-Bennett reveals in his official biography of King George VI that the King's Private Secretary, Sir Alan Lascelles, would have advised him to agree. In fact Attlee was not defeated and did not ask for a dissolution until some eighteen months later. The correspondence was brought to an end by Sir Alan under the pseudonym of 'Senex'. He laid it down that the King had an entirely personal choice whether to grant a dissolution or not. He went on to express the opinion that 'no wise sovereign' would refuse a dissolution.

'Unless he were satisfied that: (1) the existing parliament was vital, viable and capable of doing its job; (2) a general election would be detrimental to the national economy; (3) he could rely on finding another prime minister who could carry his government for a reasonable time with a working majority in the House of Commons.'

These provisos raise some interesting questions. Who is to judge whether an election in fact would be 'detrimental to the national economy'? What constitutes a 'reasonable time' for the new prime minister in the existing parliament? Would any prime minister ask for a dissolution if all three conditions obviously prevailed (if they did not the king could hardly refuse)? The answer is that, however unlikely such a request may be, it is even less likely to be made if the prime minister knows that it could be rejected.

The truth is that the power of the crown has quite properly in an era of democratic party politics become an emergency power – to find a prime minister when a national crisis arises in which the ordinary party usages prove inadequate, to guard against a reckless unnecessary general election at a time of grave economic peril, and perhaps in an extreme case to force a general election if a government for partisan purposes attempts to break the rules of the constitution and prolong itself in office. These powers are not the less important for being rarely used. It is one of the numerous tasks of the monarch's private secretary to give advice on such matters, and the prudence and wisdom which have been displayed for many years past show not only the good sense of successive monarchs but that of their hard-working, self-effacing secretaries too.

'*My husband and I always have Thursdays off!*'

Evidently the role of the monarchy is not confined to the rare exercise of emergency power. The right to be consulted, to encourage and to warn may give a prudent monarch a degree of influence far greater than a catalogue of 'powers' would suggest. Then there are those intangible, almost mystical elements in the monarchy as a symbol of national unity, detached from party controversy or affiliation in a way which no presidential head of state can ever quite be. But I doubt whether these functions could be fulfilled if all vestige of constitutional power were to disappear. If the Queen was a purely ceremonial personage and nothing else at all, her influence on ministers, and her prestige in this country and the Commonwealth would not be what they are. To answer the question with which we began, the monarch will normally 'nod his head in assent or shake it in denial as his minister pleases', and will seldom wish to do otherwise, recognizing as he does that he is a constitutional monarch whose ultimate title derives from popular support. But a residue of effective discretionary power remains, however rarely it is used. The Whigs have not had their way, as Baron Stockmar feared. The monarch is not a mandarin figure.

SASTHI BRATA

Sasthi Brata grew up as the youngest of four children in a wealthy Brahmin family in Calcutta, his father being fifty-six years old when he was born. He left home at nineteen and has lived abroad for nearly a decade, including long stretches in Paris and Copenhagen. After reading physics at university, he worked in factories, bars, petrol stations, kitchens, as crime reporter and feature writer on an Indian national daily, and for three years as a junior executive in a London engineering firm.

His autobiography *My God Died Young* and his first novel *Suspended* have recently been published. He is not yet thirty and is single.

THE JEWEL IN THE CROWN

SASTHI BRATA

The literal translation of the first two lines of the Indian National Anthem is as good a point as any from which to start talking about the British monarchy:

> 'Salutations unto thee,
> O leader of people's minds
> And arbiter of India's destiny . . . .'

The poem was written by Rabindranath Tagore just before George V visited India (for the second time) and held the Delhi Durbar as King-Emperor in 1911. Though no specific mention is made of the King in the entire poem (of which only the first stanza makes up the national anthem), the ambiguity of its phrasing provoked charges of sycophancy against its author. Tagore did not refute these charges till rather late in the day, at a time in fact when George V was no longer king and nationalist feeling in India had swelled to revolutionary proportions. At the time of Independence, when elected representatives of the people had to decide on a national anthem, a debate developed between two groups, the one which supported the liberal universal sentiments expressed in Tagore's poem and the other which was wedded to the insurrectionary words of 'Bande Mataram' – a song composed by a nineteenth-century novelist, Bankim Chatterjee, which was the seminal point round which revolutionary sentiment grew in Bengal. 'Bande Mataram' had sounded a call as historic as the 'Marseillaise' and left behind in its trail as many corpses of zealous men who rose up against oppression and tyranny. But it was the 'salutation' song which became the national anthem of Independent India.

The irony does not need to be underlined. But it is a useful springboard for a discussion of the importance and relevance of the institution of monarchy in the strife-strewn history of Empire and the Commonwealth. It is fashionable for Indian radicals of the Oxbridge mould to read the history of India's fight for independence through the rose-tinted glasses of Fabian Utopia – where the people are always in the right, and the sordid tales of exploitation the offsprings of unholy wedlock between the decadent classes of East and West. The masses were stainlessly white, the maharajahs and princes demons of the darkest hell, and India was sucked and plundered for over 200 years by a collusive syndicate of imperial whites and blacks. Gandhi awakened the dormant sense of nationhood in the Indian peoples and fanned the smouldering embers of resentment into flames of indignant rebellion; his practical-realistic techniques of non-violent resistance threw off the yoke of the British Raj. Long live India and Independence!

It is high time to take a closer look at this neat and idealistic interpretation of history.

Tickled at the weakest point of her megalomaniacal personality by Disraeli, Victoria declared herself the first British Empress of the Indian dominions. It is an unnoticed irony of history that what was essentially a domestic *political* move became in retrospect a profound act of statesmanship in preserving the Empire for as long as it lasted.

For I do not believe that the British could have remained in India after the turn of the century – if that long – had there been no British monarch to whom the Indian people could have pledged their loyalties, divorced from their anger and frustration against the political apparatus imposed upon them by an alien people.

Viewed from this perspective the Delhi Durbar was not an exercise in ostentation; it diluted the vitriolic feelings which were then brewing against the British and lubricated the passage of several awkward pieces of political legislation. The procession which welcomed the King-Emperor and his wife on their arrival in Bombay was spearheaded by

'... the Imperial insignia and a herald proclaiming in the *vernacular*, Long live Emperor George! Long live the King of Kings! Long live the Great Power!' (My italics.)

The sentiments expressed in the national anthem bear too close a resemblance for the comfort of those who would see Tagore as a knight in shining armour fighting for India's independence against the British.

In his speech of welcome to the King and his spouse, the City Father of Bombay (an Indian) said that

'... His Majesty's determination to announce his coronation in person to his Indian people was a demonstration that the crown was the living bond uniting many different races in different climes under the flag which stood for ideals of justice, toleration and progress.'

If this was merely the feeling of a fawning minority craving favours from the foreign paymasters, then it is somewhat surprising that over a quarter of a million people burst into tumultuous applause at the end of the speech.

This is how the special correspondent of *The Times* described the Durbar:

'The ceremony at its culminating point *exactly typified* the Oriental conception of the ultimate repositories of Imperial power. The Monarch sat alone, remote but beneficient, raised far above the multitude, but visible to all, clad in rich vestments, flanked by radiant emblems of authority, guarded by a glittering array of troops, the cynosure of the proudest Princes of India, the central figure in what was surely the most majestic assemblage ever seen in the East.' (Italics mine.)

It was not hard in those fulsome days to scatter priceless purple over one's prose; in mid-century Britain it is easy for an Indian to sit in the Bodleian and cast a mocking glance at such tendentious acclaim. But to see the prolonged period of British rule in the sub-continent as a direct function of both the mystique of monarchy and the Indian temperament is neither pleasant nor intellectually fashionable. For the special correspondent of *The Times* was not quite so off the mark when he wrote that the Durbar ceremony 'exactly typified' an Oriental conception of the ruler to the ruled.

It has been argued that the servile and obsequious aspect of Indian personality was the *result* of an era of oppression imposed by an alien people. To attempt to turn the argument on its head has always seemed sacrilegious to anglicized Indians and British left-wingers. But history shows that Indians, except for pocket minorities, were bowing down to their lords and masters for well over a thousand years before the British appeared on the scene. And it was only when the ruler failed to 'typify' the Oriental conception of his person that Empires broke up and internecine strife between rival factions ensued.

I am suggesting, in fact, that the Empire was finally consolidated when Queen Victoria became Empress of India as she then symbolized in the Indian mind an extra-terrestrial writ to govern mere mortals, the hand of God in human affairs, an incarnation. The idea is not as far fetched as it appears at a glance, for Gandhi, apart from being clad in the mantle of the Mahatma – saint and father of the nation – was widely regarded by 'the masses' as an incarnation; I once saw Nehru angrily *kick* a man out of his way – as he was walking down the aisle at a public meeting – because the man wanted to pay homage to the Lord Vishnu in human form. The head of the only remaining Hindu kingdom in the world, Nepal, is even now worshipped as an incarnation of the Creator of the Universe; husbands are still held to be miniature gods by their wives. When I was a child my mother used to recite to me a Sanskrit couplet whose literal translation would be:

> 'Worship thy father and thy mother,
> For they are the human forms
> Of Gods who reign high above.'

The whole fabric of Hindu society is permeated with the belief that the only sanction of authority is a divine one, that truth is *revealed* rather than the end-product of an analytic quest, and the individual is less important than the community. It would be digressive in the present context to pursue the point and show that western parliamentary democracy is notionally irrelevant in India and that it was adopted in the country to salve the consciences of Western Oriental Gentlemen who sought the applause of the *New Statesman* and the Fabian Society – perhaps unconsciously – more than the 'good' of their own people.

My concern here however is to show that the British successfully exploited this conceptual commitment of divinity through their monarchs and so established the strongest-ever colonial Empire. There is a belief floating around in certain quarters that the Raj was essentially a grand collection of fuddy-duddies who enjoyed their 'punkah and sherbet', displayed gross insensitivity to the feelings of the natives and bungled their way through 200 years of Imperial history. I suggest that this belief is a result of wishful thinking by people who cannot see human events other than in terms of white and black.

The British in India were in fact neither demons nor saints. They displayed more insight into the psychology of the native population than any other Imperial power, which did not integrate with the conquered people. As a legacy they left behind an excellent administrative service, railways, postal system, the basis of an industrial economy, a far-flung country unified for the first time in many a century – even with partition – and the seeds of the western empirical-analytic apparatus. And all this was accomplished principally in the last hundred years of British rule, the period over which the monarch was also the head of the Indian dominions. As I have tried to show earlier, I do not believe that this was mere coincidence. For even at the fiercest point of India's struggle for Independence, neither Tagore nor Gandhi – surely the two most widely revered Indians – ever disavowed their loyalty to the crown.

I am not making a value judgement. Or perhaps I should. Whatever 'good' might result as a by-product, it is always morally wrong to exploit, to govern by force, to buy a slave so you can improve his standard of living. The British did all these things and they were morally wrong in doing so. But actions which are morally repulsive do not always produce a complete spectrum of undesirable results.

I have talked so far of the mystique of monarchy in that it provided an adhesive as well as a nucleus for loyalty in the Imperial context. But the concept of divine rights was not a uniquely Oriental one; kings and queens of Europe have often used the idea as a rod with which to beat recalcitrant subjects into submission and one particularly obdurate monarch proceeded to lose his head rather than abandon his 'special relationship' with the Almighty. American slave-owners and South African ministers have sought support from the Bible in the execution of their lurid duties. Perhaps human nature and the beliefs it upholds is not all that different in different parts of the globe at different times.

But it is interesting to trace the connexion between the *raison d'être* of the monarchy from those far-off days up to the present times and to try and see how it affects our individual lives. I do

33

c

not think there is a single monarch in the world at the moment who would use the concept of divine rights to justify his role. Although King Mahendra of Nepal is, and the Emperor of Japan was, held to be descended from the gods, it is unlikely that either of them would advocate the idea as a basis for serious discussion. Certainly in the western context, if a king or queen so much as suggested that they believed in their own divinity, rapid arrangements would be made for an announcement of abdication for 'health reasons' and not less than three resident psychiatrists would be employed to keep the patient under control.

Yet in a largely secular society the monarchy still exercises a powerful fascination in the minds of people; even the most vehement anti-royalist has to admit that his desire to demolish the monarchy is provoked by the fact that 'it is there'.

When I was first asked to contribute to this symposium – the invitation came quite out of the blue – my own feelings about the monarchy were summed up in the phrase, 'What shall we do with Granny?' I was neither strongly in support nor vehemently against preserving the institution. I had never witnessed the Changing of the Guards or Trooping the Colour – except on the screen. I always switch off the goggle-box before the slow-walking Francis Chichester reaches Her Majesty. And I was faintly amused when Tommy Steele, in a recent television interview, accused the BBC of gross disloyalty for not showing the picture of 'our glorious Queen' on the set at the end of the day. Funniest of all, I was reminded of that usherette in an ABC cinema who insisted that the practice of playing the National Anthem must be continued as it helped to clear the hall of 'snogging couples' far quicker than anything else.

Granny was in fact neither wicked nor repulsive but simply rather old and faintly tedious. As far as going to work or having a pinta was concerned, she was irrelevant. If the other members of the family had angry words to say or lavished glowing tributes on her birthday, I could not be bothered to be caught up in their outbursts. I had too many other things to think and worry about.

This attitude of indifference began to undergo a subtle metamorphosis as I started gathering material for this piece and devote more thought to the subject than I had ever done before. I could not help feeling that although most Indians *in India* could not give a damn whether the Queen went or stayed, my own position as a resident in this country and holder of a British passport was, in fact, a good deal different. For in a very pervasive way the institution of monarchy does affect my personal life and therefore as a thinking human being I am obliged to have opinions about it.

I am, then, in favour of the monarchy as a political institution though my reasons would probably not bear constitutional analysis. So far as I as a member of the coloured racial minority in this country have any political allegiance, I have no choice but to be a Labour supporter. Though events in recent months[1] have woefully smudged the copy, Labour's record has been essentially one of humanity, egalitarianism and sanity. The Labour party gave India its Independence, created the Welfare State, abolished capital punishment and humanized the law governing homosexual conduct. I do not believe that any of these things could have happened under Tory rule. And because it is professedly a party of privilege, I cannot overcome the instinctive feeling that 'the Tories are out to get me', just as I have to live with the fact that the majority of the white inhabitants of these islands feel a certain animosity towards me because of the colour of my skin.

Now, this is essentially a conservative country; Labour gets into power by the back door only after long and messy periods of Tory rule. It is not inconceivable that in the next general elections, when the 'colour problem' will have become even more acute than it is now, 'to do something about it' will be a part of the Tory platform. That *something* could well be far less humane than merely shutting the door in the face of a fresh influx of coloured immigrants. I do not intend to be alarmist but I cannot rule out a frenzy of xenophobia sweeping the country. If that does happen and if the Tories are in power, the minority voice of reason within that party might well be silenced by the thundering roar of majority hate and animosity. Most, most people in this country do not like strangers, coloured strangers least of all. If democracy meant that majority opinion was put into effect on every single issue, then I *could* not be living in this country now. I do because there are sane and civilized men who believe that

[1] This essay was written shortly after an Act was passed by the Labour party, the effect of which was to deny entry into Britain to British passport-holders in Kenya.

'the masses' are not always in the right and some political decisions have to be taken in defiance of public opinion. But I *can* foresee a situation in which such sane and civilized attitudes would be over-ruled in a parliament composed largely of right-wing Tories. I have no intention of speculating on the various courses which would be considered if the 'colour situation' became bitter and violent. But it would be naïve to think that 'it could never happen here'. There might well come a time when official policy is succinctly represented by those grotesque slogans on public and lavatory walls: 'Wogs Go Home' and such like or even worse.

So if it *were* to happen and if parliament were to pass a lunatic piece of legislation in defiance of this country's long tradition of humanity and justice, I look upon the Queen as the ultimate safeguard. Perhaps she would be constitutionally powerless to intervene; or even more frightening, she might not want to. But then perhaps my feelings stem not from logic but that old Indian belief that a monarch is the *deus ex machina,* the hand of the god of justice and benevolence in human affairs.

The monarchy as an institution however is the least relevant in the political sphere. If Alf Garnett has become part of English iconology it is because such characters uphold beliefs which, in their sheer inconsistency, border on the comic. They express dark subterranean feelings of inadequacy which exist in all of us. The need to do oneself proud by parading kinship with the rich and mighty is not confined to 'the lower classes'. The moon is a shining mirror and not the less attractive to swooning couples for that reason. It is easier to be a staunch royalist supported by the Queen than a citizen of the world.

But it is hard to fix the precise point in the curve where reason lapses and the wriggling worms of subconscious mania feed our beliefs. Even in the mid-twentieth century we cannot analyse the popular appeal of the monarchy entirely in terms of function and utility. The sophisticate allows that there is an unrehearsed area of commitment with an uneasy grin. Prince Charles complains, in his university rag, of the dustman who wakes him up at five every morning with a raucous rendering of 'O come all ye faithful'. The article is reprinted in a national daily and the next day that same toneless dustman is invited to sign a contract with Pye Records. We offer the story with crisps and olives at cocktail parties. Brittle laughter and much fluttering of false eyelashes ensue. No one bothers to ask why.

For even if we concede that it is better to have a monarch than not to have one, by what logical process do we conclude that Prince Charles is better equipped to govern than a thousand other bright and handsome boys? Because he is the son of the reigning monarch and we place all our bets on the principle of heredity in order to perpetuate the mystique of monarchy. We ignore the patent contradiction between this principle and the concept of an egalitarian society.

This society accepts the idea – at least in theory – that people should be judged and rewarded on the basis of what they achieve, that the accident of birth should be neither a handicap nor an asset. The miner's son should be provided with the opportunity of entering parliament and, if he succeeds in getting there, the fact of his lowly origins should not be held against him. The duke's son does not inherit *a priori* rights to become chairman of the board. But when it comes to the monarchy the hereditary principle is accepted without question. As there is no choice, considerations of competence and merit for the job of being king do not arise. If not exactly divine, British society still considers its monarchs *above* the normal run of human beings. And because there is no rational basis for this belief we call it a mystique.

But such a mystique creates an unhealthy dialectic. We disapprove of the principle of heredity as a valid basis for social discrimination – in theory at any rate – yet at the apex of the social pyramid the monarch precisely exemplifies that very principle. And as social institutions do not exist *in vacuo,* the monarchy provides sanction to caste, the royal family is set up on a pedestal; dukes, marquesses and hereditary peers remain.

It is at this point, both as a foreigner and a socialist, that my feelings turn against the monarchy and all it symbolizes. For though I do not disapprove of a hierarchical society, I cannot accept barriers imposed by birth. It is neither fair nor efficient to prevent the boy from an East Hackney home from getting to the top of the ladder if he is so inclined and if he has the talent. Caste throttles the fertilization of ideas; no technological society can be efficiently run on such a feudal basis. And since the monarchy is exempt from judgement on the 'cost-effective' principle while its other-worldly mystique lends support to the opposite camp, it is both morally wrong and socially wasteful.

The insidious and ironic thing is that those who are most adversely affected by the institution are precisely its strongest supporters. I have to confess that I would be far more flattered to receive an invitation for lunch from Buckingham Palace than from 10 Downing Street. Yet it is theoretically conceivable that I should one day be living at Downing Street but never at the Palace. All other offices of power or prestige are theoretically accessible to me while the throne is not. It is highly unlikely that I should ever get to propose to Princess Anne and quite impossible that she should accept me even if I did. To this the most sanctified area of British society I do not and can never have any access. Therefore, like all outcasts, I have to condemn a system which shuts the door in my face.

But this is the extreme, the glittering end of the spectrum. Away from the limelight there are cabals which are just as exclusive, where caste and class provide complementary support to status. And if it is accepted that opportunities for social mobility are desirable, then an institution which upholds the opposite principle is necessarily undesirable. In this context, if British society does not *accept* me then that non-acceptance is a function of monarchy. For the social potency of a personality is proportional to the heights it can possibly climb; even a senior man who is fossilized in a post wields less power than a junior recruit with a bright and unlimited future; potential is often more attractive than partial achievement.

There has been a lot of talk in recent years about the breakdown of class in British society. And indeed in the post-war period a large number of people from the lower echelons of the social hierarchy have been absorbed into the establishment. But individual breakthroughs do not indicate general acceptance of the principle of social mobility. The old-boy network still operates; the occasional grammar-school and redbrick face in the Foreign Office enhances rather than nullifies the birthright of the upper-middle and aristocratic classes. The 'angry young man' movement in the arts was a swindle because its proponents claimed to be fighting for a whole class whereas in practice they were merely seeking personal recognition from their lords and masters. And it is no small irony that one of the most energetic

By appointment to the Prime Minister

performers in the A.Y.M. menagerie connected himself by marriage to sources very close to the Royal Family. For as long as the monarchy exists there will always be a self-perpetuating aristocracy with select rules of admission for outsiders. One cannot see how this can be reconciled with the concept of a progressive society.

Having said all this one must note that the monarchy enjoys extensive majority support. The masses do not argue, when they can worship. There seems little likelihood that in a parliamentary democracy the reigning monarch will ever be overthrown by majority vote. The throne survived an abdication and I suspect that the resiliency of the institution was even then not exhausted. It would be difficult for any monarch to do something completely to discredit both the individual as well as the institution. The machinery which produces and maintains the reigning sovereign is uniquely equipped to turn out non-controversial, innocuous and adorable personalities. And British society in the mass does not like change. So, short of military conquest by a foreign power or a gory *coup*, the monarchy will obviously remain with us as long as Big Ben chimes and the Union Jack flies at the mast-heads.

How do I feel about reconciling myself to such a situation? Well, I cannot see myself plotting an assassination or frantically lobbying the republican cause. My dreams are not strewn with vengeful thoughts about the Queen. If I am ever invited to Buckingham Palace I should certainly love to go. Royal Honours I shall accept, just as I shall consume gossip about the Royal Family with the same avid interest as millions of other Britons – and hope to God that Her Britannic Majesty continues to allow me 'to pass without let or hindrance' as she requested and required 'all those whom it may concern' to do when she gave me my passport.

JOHN GRIGG

John Grigg is a political journalist, born in 1924. He was
Captain of the Oppidans at Eton, and an Exhibitioner at
New College, Oxford, where he took a second class honours
degree in Modern History and won the Gladstone Memorial Prize for an essay on F. D. Maurice, the founder of
Christian Socialism. During the War he served with the
Grenadier Guards in Holland and Germany. In the 1951
and 1955 elections he was Tory candidate for Oldham
West. At the end of 1955 he became Lord Altrincham on
his father's death, but never sat in the House of Lords,
because of his opposition to hereditary membership of
Parliament. In 1963 he disclaimed his peerage as soon as
the law enabled him to do so. For 12 years he was associate
editor, then editor, of the *National and English Review*.
Since 1960 he has had a regular column in the *Guardian*,
besides writing intermittently for other papers. He
published *Two Anglican Essays* in 1958. He is married and
has one small son.

A SUMMER STORM

JOHN GRIGG

In 1957 I was editing a small-circulation political monthly, the *National and English Review,* and for the August issue of that year I decided to feature the monarchy. Having commissioned articles on various aspects of the subject – such as the role of the Queen's private secretary, the finances of the Royal Family, the royal palaces and art collections, and Asia's view of the Head of the Commonwealth – I wrote an introduction to the symposium, of about 4,000 words, entitled 'The Monarchy Today'. While writing it, I never for one moment suspected that it would provoke an almighty row and land me, temporarily, in the glare of world-wide publicity. Yet such was its effect, and the circumstances may now be worth recalling, if only as a footnote to history.

Readers under twenty-five will need to be informed, and some of their elders may need to be reminded, of the prevailing atmosphere at that time, so far as the monarchy was concerned – an atmosphere compounded of sycophancy and hypocrisy. The Queen succeeded her father in 1952 and her coronation the following year was the first of the television age, the first since the social revolution which began in 1940, and the first since the liquidation of the Indian Empire. Britain had undergone fundamental changes since the previous coronation in 1937, and so had the Commonwealth of which the British sovereign is nominally head. Yet the coronation was organized as though nothing much had happened. It was an interlude of solemn pretence, an orgy of make-believe, in which the mass media were in league with the most blindly conservative forces in our society.

Those invited to attend the ceremony in Westminster Abbey were mostly citizens of the United Kingdom, and by no means all of them were citizens of outstanding merit. The peerage was admitted in large numbers (though peers who were not privy councillors had to ballot for seats), while the elected parliamentarians of Commonwealth countries other than Britain were scarcely represented at all. Mr Dermot Morrah and I protested against this unimaginative use of a great occasion, but to no avail. The British authorities were not interested in change, and the then Canadian High Commissioner (Mr Norman Robertson) was content to leave all the arrangements to the Duke of Norfolk.

Meanwhile the Queen was being 'sold' to the people not just as a figure of romance (which, by the nature of her office, she certainly was and is), but as an almost hieratic figure. The speeches written for her were impersonal sermons of immense condescension, and she was encouraged to see herself as a sort of high priestess, embodying the moral and spiritual qualities, if not the actual powers, attributed to the monarchy in the heyday of divine right. Politicians and other members of the state establishment were at her feet. As Prime Minister, the veteran Winston Churchill treated her with the autumnal chivalry of Melbourne and an unction more genuine than Disraeli's. The clergy grovelled, and so – most regrettably – did the press.

Editors and broadcasters were to a large extent victims of their own propaganda. Forgetting that the traditional British attitude towards the monarchy is loyal and (whenever possible) affectionate, but definitely not servile, they acted on the assumption that the public shared the official, quasi-religious view of the Queen. Very little criticism of any kind appeared, and such as did appear was directed, not at the Queen herself or her relations, but at their entourage. The general tone of the press was meek and reverent to a degree which would not now be credited, but which was thought to correspond with the popular mood. Actually, the people, though slightly bemused, had not on the whole lost their sense of proportion – as events were to show.

The moratorium on truth lasted for a good five years after the Queen's accession. Much of the nonsense spoken and written about the Royal Family during that period was, of course, perfectly sincere, though much of it was disingenuous. In an industry which depends upon advertisement revenue the supposed prejudices of the admass are not readily affronted. But whatever its motivation, the royal 'copy' of the period makes strange reading today. An article by Sir Arthur Bryant, published in the *Sunday Times* on November 6, 1955, may be judged the prize exhibit. Sir Arthur's good faith is not in doubt; when he writes of personalities in the English saga his heart is usually stronger than his head. On this occasion he was writing of Princess Margaret who, after a fortnight's highly publicized vacillation, had just decided against marrying Group-Captain Peter Townsend.

The reason given for her renunciation was that her duty to the Commonwealth and the Church of England took precedence over her private happiness. Those who knew her best tended to see her action in a rather less heroic light, but Sir Arthur accepted it at face value, without a flicker of scepticism, and made it the theme of an historical rhapsody in which he compared her, by implication, to Queen Elizabeth I, Thomas Becket, Nelson, Florence Nightingale and Scott of the Antarctic. Her decision, he said, 'was an act of history, and one that will not be without its effect on the future of our time'. Thirteen years later its cosmic importance eludes us, but it can safely be said that no such article would appear nowadays in the *Sunday Times,* or in any other serious British newspaper.

Against that background, I should like to summarize what I wrote in August, 1957, as the article was read by only a small minority of those who took an interest in the subsequent controversy. As a result, my basic position has been – and is still – very widely misunderstood. By some I am condemned, by others praised, as a republican, whereas in fact I am a pretty ardent monarchist. For better or worse, my article was intended as a small service to a great institution in which I believe.

I began by attempting to describe those ways in which the British monarchy had successfully adapted itself to the new age. 'The decisive reign was that of George V. When he came to the Throne the Royal Family was still more German than British . . . The Kaiser's war put an end to this . . . it also gave a dramatic impetus to social and political change in this country. George V was not a clever man and his constitutional sense was sometimes defective, yet his services to the monarchy are beyond price, since he managed to adjust it, in essentials, to the new conditions.'

By the end of his reign the Commonwealth was beginning to take shape and, at home, the upper class was losing ground. Yet the monarchy was holding its own. 'The reasons for this strange development are complex, but the significance of the King's own character can hardly be exaggerated. Unlike his father, he was not fashionable or a pleasure-seeker; he was never regarded as belonging to what is loosely called "society". He typified the virtues and limitations of millions of his subjects, and there was thus a natural sympathy between him and them, which his mastery of the new technique of sound broadcasting helped to confirm. What Baldwin did for parliamentary government, George V did for the monarchy.'

His second son inherited some of his qualities, showed 'exactly the right demeanour in 1940', and by his marriage brought native British blood into the Royal Family. 'But this is a point not to be laboured, because the monarchy must not now be exclusively British; it must transcend race.' The Duke of Edinburgh, 'whose merits are almost universally extolled, is British only by adoption' and 'gives the impression of being a citizen of the Commonwealth, at home wherever he goes.' He thus shows himself to be aware of 'the new pattern within which the monarchy must work – and "work" is the word – in the difficult years ahead.'

There was much to admire in the present Royal Family, but 'it would be a disastrous mistake to feel anything like complacency about their hold upon the allegiance of the mass public, especially in those parts of the Commonwealth which are not British.' The coronation had induced a mood 'which of its very nature was superficial and impermanent'. The monarchy would not survive, let alone thrive, 'unless its leading figures exert themselves to the full and with all the imagination they and their advisers can command.'

Before passing on to specific criticisms I took a swipe at the crypto-republicanism which lurked behind a façade of devotion to the throne. 'The Whig magnates ignored or despised the Royal Family, but exalted the institution of monarchy. Nowadays the position is reversed. Many influential people, of varying political opinions, are able to combine a high regard for the Royal Family with a fundamental scepticism as to the viability of the institution.' As republics were now the rule, and monarchies very much the exception, anyone who asserted that the British monarchy would endure was not stating a self-evident proposition; he was almost saying *credo quia impossibile*.

The passages which followed were those which the world press chose to quote. 'When she has lost the bloom of youth the

Queen's reputation will depend, far more than it does now, upon her personality. It will not then be enough for her to go through the motions . . .' The monarchy had to transcend class as well as race. Social distinctions were inevitable, but 'the crown must not seem to be identified with any particular social group.' Unfortunately the relatively classless character of George V was not reproduced in his grand-daughters. 'The Queen and Princess Margaret still bear the debutante stamp.'

Why? 'The most likely reason is that they were given a conventional upper-class education . . . "Crawfie", Sir Henry Marten, the London season, the racecourse, the grouse moor, Canasta, and the occasional royal tour – all this would not have been good enough for Queen Elizabeth I! It says much for the Queen that she has not been incapacitated for her job by this woefully inadequate training. She has dignity, a sense of duty and (so far as one can judge) goodness of heart – all precious assets. But will she have the wisdom to give her children an education very different from her own? Will she, above all, see to it that Prince Charles is equipped with all the knowledge he can absorb without injury to his health, and that he mixes during his formative years . . . not merely with future landowners or stockbrokers?'

While it was not legitimate to criticize the Queen's choice of strictly private friends, it was 'quite in order to criticize public functions, such as the presentation parties, which are a grotesque survival' from the past. Moreover, one was entitled to deplore the composition of the royal household, which emphasized the 'social lopsidedness' to which the monarchy was still prone. 'The Queen's entourage . . . are almost without exception people of the "tweedy" sort.' Such people might have many merits, but as a group they were unrepresentative. 'Worse still, courtiers are nearly always citizens of one Commonwealth country – the United Kingdom . . . while the monarchy has become "popular" and multi-racial, the Court has remained a tight little enclave of British "ladies and gentlemen" . . . The Queen should surely now be surrounded by advisers and companions with as many different backgrounds as possible.'

The advent of broadcasting had given a new importance to the spoken word, and George V had made excellent use of the opportunity so provided. George VI had done his best, though handicapped. The Duke of Edinburgh was proving himself 'a first-rate speaker', not least on television – a medium to which 'the Royal Family, like all others who are engaged in public life, will have to pay increasing attention.'

After noting that the Queen's Christmas broadcast would, that year, for the first time be televised, I felt it necessary to comment rather sharply on the style and content of her speeches (though not, as many quite mistakenly inferred, on her voice). 'She will not ... achieve good results with her present style of speaking, which is frankly "a pain in the neck". Like her mother, she appears to be unable to string even a few sentences together without a written text ... Phrases such as "I am deeply moved" sound very hollow when they are read from a typescript. But even if the Queen feels compelled to read all her speeches, great and small, she must at least improve her method of reading them. With practice, even a prepared text can be given an air of spontaneity.'

The subject matter should also, I suggested, be conceived in a quite different spirit – a spirit appropriate to the speaker. George V did not write his own speeches, but 'they seemed to be a natural emanation from, and expression of, the man'. By contrast, the Queen's speeches were totally unsuited to her character. 'The personality conveyed by the utterances which are put into her mouth is that of a priggish schoolgirl, captain of the hockey team, a prefect, and a recent candidate for Confirmation.' (N.B., I did not say that she *was* a priggish schoolgirl, etc. On the contrary, my point was that her real character was being hidden behind a mask of synthetic regality and sacerdotal pomposity.)

In conclusion, I tried to conjure up a picture of what the monarchy could achieve in the modern world. 'If it can become popular in the fullest sense, without losing its romantic appeal ... it will deserve a place among the wonders of the world. To be popular it need not descend to the petty bicycle-riding showmanship which some monarchs consider necessary to keep themselves in business; its gestures must not be superficial ... Nor need the Royal Family become a tribe of nomads in order to fulfil their mission in the Commonwealth.' They should certainly 'reside more in countries other than the United Kingdom', but this did not mean that they should be perpetually on the move. 'When they arrive somewhere it must not always be to the accompaniment of flags and fireworks and addresses of welcome, but rather like the moon and stars in Coleridge's incomparable description: "... that still sojourn, yet still move onward; and everywhere the blue sky belongs to them, and is their appointed rest, and their native country and their own natural homes, which they enter unannounced, as lords that are certainly expected, and yet there is a silent joy at their arrival".'

On Saturday, August 3rd, the *Daily Express* ran as its main front-page story most of the critical passages from the article, together with some complimentary remarks about me (attributed to 'friends') and a leader denouncing the article as 'vulgar' and 'destructive'. This ambivalent treatment was typical of much press reaction during the early days. Several other national newspapers carried reports on the Saturday, but hundreds more – at home and abroad – joined in over the weekend, which happened to be the weekend of August bank holiday. This I spent in relative peace and seclusion with friends in Sussex, but when I got back to London on the Monday evening I found reporters waiting outside my flat, and the door could hardly be opened for the pile of letters inside.

For the next few weeks life was indescribably hectic. The telephone rang incessantly (I was even woken in the small hours by a call from Australia). With every post wads of letters thumped through my letter-box – over 2,000 in the first week. Many were abusive and some threatening, but at least half of them were sympathetic, even at the outset. Reporters and photographers dogged my footsteps. My name was soon a household word, becoming part of the stock-in-trade of commentators and comedians, and falling upon my ears wherever I went – in shops, in trains, in the street. Even when the immediate rumpus subsided, I remained, as it were, in a state of over-exposure for many months, even years, and the experience has given me some idea what it must be like to be a political leader or a pop idol.

The immense reverberations of the article were not, of course, due exclusively, or even primarily, to its merits (although I venture to think it had some). An earlier attack by Malcolm Muggeridge on what he called the 'royal soap opera' had created only a mild flutter. My criticisms were, perhaps, more specific and more serious, but what made them particularly newsworthy was that they came from an unexpected quarter. At that time I was a peer, having inherited my father's peerage in 1955. I was also an old Etonian, had served in the Brigade of Guards, and had twice stood for Parliament as a Tory. In the crude philosophy of gossip columnists and class determinists I was an unlikely person to criticize the Queen. My title and antecedents, if not my real self, were good material for a Fleet Street pantomime.[1]

There was certainly a strong element of vaudeville in the row which developed. I was anathematized by the Archbishop of Canterbury, threatened by various backwoodsmen with shooting, horse-whipping, or hanging, drawing and quartering, slapped by an elderly member of the League of Empire Loyalists, and challenged to a duel by an Italian monarchist, Commendatore Marmirolli (who a year later, when I was in Rome for my honeymoon, made amends by presenting my wife with two dozen roses, with the assurance that he had come to recognize me as a true monarchist after all). There was a move to expel me from one of my clubs, and it was even rumoured that I might be struck off the list of Old Etonians, though the cost of reprinting, apparently, deterred those who wished to inflict this meaningless punishment.

While I was determined not to withdraw what I had said, since I believed it to be true and worth saying, I was anxious to keep the controversy within bounds. The scale and character of the publicity disturbed me, and I was most unwilling to be associated for life with one subject, and one subject only. I therefore refused countless invitations to write follow-up articles on the monarchy and appealed – though without much success – for a period of calm.

It was most important, however, that I should have the chance to defend myself on British television, and that chance would have been denied me had the BBC monopoly still been in force. Gagged by the BBC, on Tuesday, August 6th, I was interviewed for ITN by Robin Day, and later that week answered on Granada

---

[1] The automatic newsworthiness of peers had an unfortunate effect during the controversy, when the *New Statesman* (of all papers) printed a letter from Lord Londonderry, a very young peer with a certain talent for jazz-playing. He referred to the Royal Family's 'deplorable taste in clothes', and made a number of other comments, which seemed to me both mistaken and trivial, but which nevertheless 'rubbed off' on me. Lord Londonderry soon recanted, but the harm was done.

questions put to me by a group of young people. Those
appearances, and a filmed interview for Pathé News, probably
did more than anything else to make my argument and its true
motivation known to the general public. Just before I left home
to be questioned by Robin Day, the late Bill Connor ('Cassandra'
of the *Daily Mirror*) spoke to me on the telephone. 'I thought
you'd like to know,' he said, 'that our readers' letters are now
supporting you in a ratio of thirteen to four.' The news was indeed
heartening, as it more than confirmed the evidence of my own
postbag. By the end of the week there had been a further shift
of mass opinion in my direction, as four out of five *Mirror*
letters were by then supporting me.

Meanwhile the Chief Metropolitan Magistrate, in passing
judgment on the man who hit me, had gratuitously observed that
95 per cent of the British people were offended by what I had
written. It was soon demonstrated that his remark was as
inaccurate as it was unjudicial. On August 12th the *Daily Mail*
published a National Opinion Poll which showed that 35 per cent
of all questioned agreed with my criticisms as a whole, with 52
per cent disagreeing. On the education of Prince Charles I had
the support of 33 per cent (against 47 per cent), and on the composition of the royal household 55 per cent supported me
(against 21 per cent). Moreover, in the Queen's own age group –
sixteen to thirty-four – my criticisms as a whole had the support
of a majority (47 per cent against 39 per cent). While there could
be nothing conclusive about those figures, they could not be
lightly dismissed. It was obvious that my views, far from being
almost universally execrated, were in fact very widely shared.

Apart from the strain of it all, I was never down-hearted,
because my friends stood by me throughout and gave me the
greatest moral support, though not all of them could agree with
me on the points at issue. One or two of them attacked my views
in public, while abating none of their kindness to me in private.
That was just as it should be, because in a civilized country it
must always be possible for friends to disagree with some
asperity on matters of public policy without damage to their
friendship.

It was reported to me that the Queen's first reaction was to
assume I must be mad, whereas Prince Philip saw at once that
the criticism should be taken seriously. If the Queen was

incredulous, who could blame her? She had been treated, since her accession, to such a concentrated dose of flattery, not to say worship, that she must indeed have been surprised to find herself the butt of criticism. I was sorry to have to hurt her feelings, but a continuation of the infallibility cult would in the long run have inflicted much graver hurt. The British monarchy has survived because it is not a sacred institution, but one which depends, like every other British institution, upon popular approval. Someone had to re-assert the traditional principle that our sovereigns are not above criticism, and that task happened to fall to me.

The idea had got around that the sovereign could never be criticized, because the Constitution provided that there was always someone else to take the rap. That was entirely false doctrine, overdue for correction. A constitutional monarchy is certainly one in which most of the powers of the state are exercised by ministers responsible to the people's elect. But the sovereign retains freedom of action wherever those powers are not involved (as Sir Robert Peel found when he tried to appoint Queen Victoria's ladies of the bedchamber). The royal household is in no sense responsible for the Queen's activities: on the contrary she is responsible for the royal household. Moreover, she is undoubtedly free to plan a large part of her programme of work. She has many opportunities to look into things for herself, and to give encouragement to her subjects, without transgressing the constitutional limits. If too little use is made of those opportunities the blame must be hers, and it must also be hers if her personal staff is inadequate.

I had to meet the further argument that the Queen should not be criticized because she could not answer back. Those who argued thus were, I felt, mistaking a privilege for a penalty. The truth was not that the Queen was obliged to remain silent under criticism, but rather that she was under no obligation to answer back – a privilege not enjoyed by, for instance, ministers of the crown, who would often be glad of its protection. That the nation's highest office-holder, being immune from the necessity to answer critics, should on that account be immune from criticism, seemed to me an argument of the purest absurdity.

So I did not apologize for my article, but defended it to the best of my ability against all comers, maintaining that the Queen

– like any other man or woman in our public life – must be open to criticism, and that my own criticisms were just.

After more than a decade it is hard to believe that my remarks could have generated so much heat. Since then the wave of satire has swept over Britain, leaving no institution or public personality unscathed. Nor have the satirists shown much pity for their victims, or much desire to improve the institutions they have attacked. For the most part they have indulged in reckless denigration and heartless ridicule. The general public, which did not wholly succumb to the earlier mood of adulation, has probably not been too deeply affected by the satirical mood. But the atmosphere has very markedly changed, on the whole for the better.

Meanwhile there have been a few changes on the monarchical front. The presentation parties were abolished in the autumn of 1957. Some non-UK (even, one might say, non-U) people have been attached to the royal household. The successor appointed in 1967 to Commander Richard Colville as Press Secretary to the Queen, is an Australian. All the same, the complexion of the Court is still very much as it used to be.

The education of Prince Charles has shown the most striking departure from traditional habits. Instead of being instructed by tutors at Buckingham Palace, he was sent away to school – and to a comparatively off-beat public school. More important, he had a spell in Australia, which he obviously much enjoyed. From all accounts he is a naturally gregarious young man, at ease in the most varied company. It is perhaps a pity that he did not attend a state primary school, and that he has been subjected to a somewhat eccentric university career. But there is much to be thankful for in the way his parents have chosen to have him educated.

The content of the Queen's speeches is now slightly less impersonal than in the early years of her reign. In her 1967 Christmas broadcast she referred to several people, including her husband, by name. Yet it has to be admitted that her public utterances still do her very much less than justice, since they largely conceal those warm human qualities which her friends admire. She hardly ever speaks, even on less formal occasions, without a prepared text, and she has never acquired the knack of reading a prepared text with liveliness or any appearance of spontaneity.

In general, she is not good at responding with animation and warmth to a popular greeting, or even to a small child presenting her with a bunch of flowers. She seems to wave, smile and accept favours in a predetermined manner, and with a deliberately self-imposed restraint, as if it were undignified to show surprise or enthusiasm. The Queen Mother and the Duke of Edinburgh are both in their different ways star performers in public, but some people count it for virtue in the Queen that she is so undemonstrative. Why, they ask, should she be expected to behave like an actress? The answer is that any public figure must to some extent cultivate the histrionic art. There is no disgrace in doing so, since even in private life what we call good manners necessitate a certain distortion of nature, an artificial conditioning of human conduct. A polite person may be fundamentally good – indeed, politeness is a shallow quality without a good character to back it – but moral worth is not diminished, and may well be enhanced, by artificial graces.

What is true in the private sphere is even more true in the public. The great world is even more of a stage than the little world in which most people pass their lives. Celebrities of all kinds have to learn a little stagecraft if they are to make the most of their parts. A queen must be sincere: she must believe in what she is doing and saying. She must also be natural in the sense that her words and actions must reflect her own personality. But neither her sincerity nor her natural merits will be fully appreciated unless they are conveyed with some of the actress's art.

On solemn occasions the Queen shows consummate dignity. But most occasions, even in the Queen's programme, are not entirely solemn, and an excessive preoccupation with dignity can at times be self-defeating. The British monarchy has such prestige that the Queen need not be asking herself at every turn 'Am I being dignified?' She can afford to take large liberties, to break conventional rules, to back her own hunch, and the accumulated credit of her office will carry her through. For all her excellence in other ways, the Queen has yet to grasp that cardinal truth.

The basic royal routine has changed very little. When the Queen travels, either within the country or outside it, her programme is almost invariably planned months in advance, and is

Ship of State, 1969

carried out in a very stylized manner. She pays few unscheduled visits to schools, hospitals, clubs, factories, or other centres of life and work. As a result, she very seldom sees the world as it really is. No one in his right senses would suggest that she should eliminate from her programme the great colourful ceremonies which people enjoy. But there is also, surely, a need for more informal, unexpected activities – and the need is certainly not met by Buckingham Palace lunch parties and cocktail parties, at which the most ill-assorted people are brought together on the naïve assumption that the Queen is kept abreast of the nation's multifarious life by a brief exchange of pleasantries with (for example) a civil servant, a sculptor, a tycoon, a footballer and a social worker.

The royal holidays, which are very long by normal standards, are still spent in the traditional UK retreats, Windsor, Sandringham and Balmoral. The Queen has no homes in other Commonwealth countries, and a vital opportunity has thus been missed. It may now be too late to give the Crown a more than symbolic meaning in those independent nations of the Commonwealth, other than Britain, which are still, technically, monarchies. Royal tours are no substitute for periods of residence; yet to most Commonwealth citizens, and to many who are actually her subjects, the Queen is only a tourist. How much does she mean, as a human being, to the people of Canada or Australia, of Ceylon or Jamaica – countries of which she is the legal sovereign? And how much has she meant to people from Commonwealth countries, especially the so-called 'coloured immigrants', who have been trying to make their homes here in recent years? Can it honestly be said that she has made anything like adequate use of the resources of initiative, inspiration and influence which belong uniquely to the monarchy, to counteract the poison of racialism which has been spreading in our midst? Unfortunately her contribution in this respect has been negligible.

To be thoroughly successful, constitutional monarchy must be more than a symbol. Lacking direct political power, it is nevertheless richly endowed with the power of example – the power to win hearts and fire the imagination. Those of us who believe in the British monarchy, not just as a symbol of stability and continuity, but as a positive force for good in the world, will not be content until it is exploiting that power to the full.

WILLIAM HAMILTON

William Hamilton has been Labour Member of Parliament for West Fife since 1950. He was born in 1917, the son of a Durham miner. He was educated at Washington Grammar School, Co. Durham, and Sheffield University, after which he became a schoolmaster and lectured on the British constitution. He has travelled to West Africa, Russia, the USA and Canada on Parliamentary business. He became Chairman of the House of Commons Estimates Committee in 1964 and in 1966 was elected Vice-Chairman of the Labour Party. He has been a consistent critic of monarchy in the House of Commons.

THE CROWN, THE CASH, AND THE FUTURE

WILLIAM HAMILTON

Sir Charles Petrie is one among many apologists for the royal *status quo* when he asserts that 'the nation makes an annual profit on the monarchy'. This remarkable conclusion is arrived at by doing some phoney arithmetic – by adding the total of the Civil List to the payments made to other members of the Royal Family, and substracting that sum from the amounts paid into the Exchequer from the revenues of the crown estate and the Duchy of Cornwall. Sir Charles and others like him seem to be arguing that monarchy is one of our most successful nationalized industries.

Not all writers agree on the point. Mr Kingsley Martin contends it is a 'legal fiction' that the crown lands, in central London and elsewhere, 'belong' to the monarch, and are voluntarily surrendered to the Exchequer at the beginning of each reign in return for the Civil List. And eighty years ago, Mr S. M. Davidson (*The New Book of Kings*) was writing, 'Before the Norman William landed in England there was hardly a manor or ecclesiastical benefice in the country that he had not by anticipation apportioned among himself and his fellows. His own share, to be sure, was a handsome one, and though repeatedly confiscated and largely alienated, the crown lands were still of considerable value at the Revolution of 1688. If they ever did belong to the kings of England as individuals – that is to say, as private estates – they completely lost that character when James II fled to France. They then reverted to the nation, and parliament, as representing the nation, used them as it had a mind. The pretence that the Guelphs have some personal right to the duchies of Lancaster and Cornwall, from which they are permitted to draw large revenues, is as hollow as their more general claim to all crown lands. The crown lands are in the strictest sense national lands, and ought, for the sake of accuracy and clearness, to be always so designated. Any revenue accruing to royalty from such sources is contributed by the nation as surely as if it arose from the tax on tea or on tobacco. It is important to remember this, as apologists of the monarchy have succeeded in breeding considerable confusion in the public mind on the subject.'

But first let us bring the arithmetic up to date. The Civil List is known. It was fixed by Parliament at £475,000 a year in 1952, at the beginning of the reign. The 'wage freeze' has been in operation since then. No doubt it was this fact which caused Dorothy Laird (*How The Queen Reigns*, 1959) to lament 'She has problems of finance, but they are not the same as those from which most of us suffer, or rather, they are on a vastly different scale.'

To the Civil List must be added the salaries paid to other royal personages – £40,000 a year to Prince Philip, £70,000 a year to the Queen Mother, £35,000 a year to the Duke of Gloucester, £15,000 a year to Princess Margaret – a total of £160,000 – most of it tax free. All these sums are provided from the Consolidated Fund, that is to say, voted annually without debate in parliament, and paid for out of general taxation.

Similarly, the cost of the upkeep of the royal palaces – Buckingham Palace, St James's Palace, Windsor Castle, Kensington Palace, Hampton Court Palace, and Holyrood House – is provided for in the vote of the Minister of Public Building and Works. The estimate for 1967-8 is £881,000. This figure includes £97,000 for staff salaries, £600,000 for building and engineering services, and £107,000 for fuel, gas and electricity, etc. In 1964-5 the gas bill amounted to £13,483, the electricity bill to £31,365, and the fuel bill to £47,522. On the housing of Princess Margaret and her husband alone, a total of £5,228 was spent on Number 10 Kensington Palace between 1960 and 1962, and another £72,600 on her present home at 1a Kensington Palace. In view of the fact that thousands of families in London and elsewhere are homeless, such expenditure is socially squalid, wholly indefensible, and shows the most reprehensible insensitivity on the part of the royal recipients.

Then there are such trivial matters as the cost of the Queen's flight of aircraft. That consists of three Andovers, one Chipmunk and two Whirlwind helicopters. According to the Ministry of Defence, the capital cost was £1.2 millions, and the current annual cost about £390,000. The only members of the Royal Family entitled to unrestricted use of these aircraft are

H.M. The Queen, Prince Philip, and the Queen Mother. But they can also be used by other members of the Royal Family, by senior ministers, and VIP's such as visiting royalty and chiefs of staff of the armed forces.

Much has been written about the royal yacht *Britannia*. Its building and fitting out costs were £2¼ millions. When in service her crew consists of 22 officers and 258 ratings, but when in harbour this is reduced to fifteen officers and 175 ratings; these cost £7,700 and £5,500 per week respectively. The average annual fuel cost is £21,000. Assuming the average weekly cost of the crew to be £6,000, the total annual cost of running the vessel must be about £330,000. But these figures do not include the cost of the two refits of the last five years. The first refit from April to June 1962, cost £60,500. The second, from December 1964 to April 1965, which included the Quadrennial Survey, cost £260,400. The justification for this expenditure is officially that *Britannia* is still capable of being used as a hospital ship in time of war, and in peacetime she provides basic training in all matters naval for her officers and men. Below is the detail of the number of occasions over the last five years on which Britannia has been used by members of the Royal Family, the reasons, and the relevant dates:

OCCASION	DATES	ROYAL FAMILY MEMBERS
Visit to the Mediterranean	April 17–29, 1961	Queen Mother
Visit to the Mediterranean	April 29–May 7, 1961	Queen and Duke of Edinburgh
Visit to the Mediterranean	May 5–May 25, 1961	Duke and Duchess of Gloucester
Visit to Aberdeen	July 31—August 14, 1961	Queen and Duke of Edinburgh
Mediterranean Cruise	February 12–March 28, 1962	Princess Royal
Visit to Scilly Isles	April 26–28, 1962	Queen Mother
Visit to West of England	July 25–27, 1962	Queen and Duke of Edinburgh
Visit to Australia and New Zealand	February 1–May 6, 1963	Queen
Visit to Channel Islands	May 8–13, 1963	Queen and Queen Mother
Visit to Isle of Man	July 4–9, 1963	Queen and Queen Mother
Visit to Cowes	August 5–9, 1963	Duke of Edinburgh
Visit to Caribbean	March 12–April 1, 1964	Queen Mother

OCCASION	DATES	ROYAL FAMILY MEMBERS
Visit to Scotland and Iceland	June 26–July 3, 1964	Queen and Duke of Edinburgh
Visit to Newfoundland	September 11–29, 1964	Princess Royal
Visit to Canada, West Indies and Caribbean	October 5– December 2, 1964	Queen and Duke of Edinburgh
Visit to Amsterdam and Hamburg	May 13–30, 1965	Queen, Duke and Princess Margaret
Visit to Isle of Wight and Clyde	August 8–16, 1965	Queen
Visit to West Indies	February 1– March 6, 1966	Queen and Duke of Edinburgh
Visit to Fiji and New Zealand	April 4–May 4, 1966	Queen Mother

This information, supplied by the Ministry of Defence, shows that the yacht was used for a total of 337 days in five years – and a large proportion of that time was clearly spent on pleasure jaunts at the public expense.

If one adds the cost of the royal train, royal postage, telegrams, telephones, all of which fall on the taxpayer quite apart from the figures mentioned above, it becomes apparent that Anthony Sampson's estimate of £2 millions a year as the cost of the monarchy to the state is very much of an underestimate.

Seen in the context of a national income of something like £30,000 millions or an annual budget of well over £9,000 millions, even £5 millions would look trifling. Seen in the context of millions of our people existing on less than £10 a week, and at least half a million children suffering the direst poverty, the crown seems to many to be a vulgar extravagance, made not less so by those who seek to prove that it is a sound national investment, by relating the cost of the income surrendered from the crown estate.

The Report of the Crown Estate Commissioners for the year ended March 31, 1966, illustrates one point apparently over-looked by the apologists. The commissioners emphasize the increasing importance of the crown's ownership of the 'foreshore and seabed', especially now that its value is increasing due to 'the construction or improvement of docks and harbours and the laying of pipelines on the bed of the sea within the crown's proprietary jurisdiction, which extends to the limit of territorial waters'. The Report particularly mentions the new pipelines

62

needed to bring ashore North Sea gas, and the commissioners make it quite clear that they 'should act commercially'; indeed, they are bound to do so *by statute*. But 'by far the most remunerative use of the seabed for the crown estate remains the extraction of sand and gravel ... Growing in importance as other sources of supply become more difficult'.

These extracts reveal the true nature of the myth of the surrender of the revenues from the crown estate as a magnanimous gesture by the sovereign. So far as is known, no one ever suggested that the pollution of the beaches in the south-west by the wreck of the oil tanker *Torrey Canyon* should be a charge on the crown estate.

The accounts of the commissioners show gross revenue receipts of over £5 millions, and the surplus revenue paid to the exchequer as £3,525,000. Thus, even assuming that Sir Charles Petrie and others are right, it would be doubtful if, when all the figures are collated, on both sides of the ledger, a profit to the state would be shown. And even if they did so, that would not be the end of the story. At least three others matters must be taken into account:

1. No estate duty is payable on the crown estate. If it had been payable over the years, the estate would long ago have been decimated.

2. Over the last century in particular, the value of urban and to a lesser extent agricultural properties has rocketed, especially in London. The gross revenues from the crown estate at the time of surrender in 1760 was £89,000. Today the figure is over £5 millions. The changing value of money makes any worthwhile comparison difficult. But there can be little doubt that the enormously increased value of the estate has been due primarily to (a) protection from erosion by estate duty, and (b) public expenditure and investment in the form of the provision of such public services as drainage and sanitation, police, roads, lighting, etc., all of which have contributed to the growth of London as a world-famous commercial, financial, and governmental centre.

3. Not all the revenues from the crown estate are handed over. Specifically those of the Duchies of Lancaster and of Cornwall are not. The annual accounts of the Duchy of Lancaster

are made available to parliament. The Chancellor of the Duchy of Lancaster is a government minister who can and does answer questions in the House of Commons on the affairs of the Duchy. That being so, it is difficult to maintain with any seriousness that the estates of the Duchy are private in any legal sense. But if they are, then why are the revenues not handed over to the state in the same way as those from others parts of the crown estate? Or does the generosity of the sovereign stop at Lancaster and Cornwall? For the year ended September 1966, £261,584 was collected in rents in the Duchy of Lancaster, of which £163,227 was for farm rents. Another £73,797 was 'The Produce of Devolution and Forfeitures'. (Devolutions are cast or property which goes direct to H.M. The Queen from certain persons who die intestate in the Duchy, within the terms of the Administration of Estates Act, 1925. The Forfeitures referred to are fines imposed or recognisances forfeited by Lancashire residents at Courts of Assize or Quarter Sessions. Total receipts of the Duchy are shown as £543,706. Out of this, £200,000 are paid direct to Her Majesty. This figure is kept more or less stable each year.)

So far as the tax liability of the crown is concerned, the Crown Estates Act of 1862 provides that the same taxes shall be paid on those properties as would be payable if they were in other ownership than that of the crown. That Act is still in force. But there is no similar provision regarding any other property of the crown or the Duchy of Lancaster. Mr Kingsley Martin refers in his book to an incident which occurred in 1959, when the Inland Revenue appeared to be overruled by some person or persons unnamed when it was proposed to tax some mining profits of some lead mines in Derbyshire which formed part of the Duchy of Lancaster. A request from the author of this essay to the Treasury to trace the incident drew a blank. The Treasury was unable to give any information on the matter. But it was emphasized that the Inland Revenue has no discretionary powers in taxation collection. This would seem to bear out Mr Martin's contention that none of the £200,000 which the Queen receives annually from the Duchy of Lancaster is taxable. Two-hundred thousand pounds tax-free each year is like hitting the football pools jackpot three or four times every season. 'Such stuff as dreams are made of!'

The revenues of the Duchy of Cornwall are presumably also tax free. Ever since 1337, when the Duchy was originated by Edward III for the support of his eldest son the Black Prince, the eldest son of the sovereign has succeeded to the dukedom by inheritance. In 1951-2 the net revenues of the Duchy amounted to about £90,000. They must be considerably more now. Of this sum, the Duke of Cornwall was to receive one-ninth (i.e. £10,000) a year until his eighteenth birthday. From the age of eighteen to twenty-one the Duke – now Prince Charles – was to get an increase to £30,000 a year. After the age of twenty-one, the entire revenues of the Duchy will accrue to him. Making the not unreasonable assumption that H.M. Queen Elizabeth reigns for another thirty years, and that the revenues of the Duchy of Cornwall remain as low as £100,000 a year, by the time Prince Charles succeeded to the throne, he would have amassed a private fortune of not less than £3 millions. As Mr R. A. Butler said in the House of Commons at the time (July 9, 1952): 'I trust that provision on this scale will be thought to be suitable.' And the House agreed.

Not only so. It was decided then – 1952 – that after the Duke of Cornwall had attained his majority he should 'reasonably be expected to make provision for his wife during their joint lives from the net revenues of the Duchy'. But that in the event of the Duke predeceasing his wife, the widow should draw £30,000 a year from the Consolidated Fund, i.e. from the poor hard-pressed taxpayer. That is what is now called long-term planning. Obviously the Conservative party sometimes accept this concept.

One further provision of the 1952 Civil List merits some mention. Any son of H.M.The Queen will receive £10,000 a year on attaining the age of twenty-one, increased to £25,000 on marriage. Equivalent rates for daughters are £6,000 and £15,000. Equal pay is not accepted at the Palace either. These provisions have been more or less the same since 1910. The only innovation in 1952 was that Princess Margaret was to receive £6,000 a year at the age of twenty-one, and a further £9,000 a year on marriage. So the playgirl Princess now receives more than the Prime Minister, and much more than any cabinet minister.

The debate on the 1952 Civil List lasted only seven hours.

Since that date fifteen years ago no further debate has been or can be allowed on the subject. Mr Attlee, then leader of the Labour opposition, proposed that there should be provision for a review of the Civil List, and presumably a debate at intervals of not longer than ten years. The idea was rejected by the government of the day, on the grounds that a constitutional monarchy should be above politics. The real reasons for the rejection were probably very different. Even a ten-yearly debate would throw too much light in too many dark places. It is politic to maintain a stern, discreet silence on an institution about which so many embarrassing questions might be asked and so many startling revelations made. The continued existence of the monarchy depends far more than any other of our institutions on a conspiracy of silence and on the aura of mystery, myth, and humbug with which it is surrounded. The continuous brainwashing of the plebs, in the schools, in the churches, in the press, and on the radio and television, creates an atmosphere of adoring stupefaction. As a nation, we have forsaken God for Elizabeth II, with Prince Philip as a latter day John the Baptist. The ordinary citizen can watch and listen to open discussions on abortion, homosexuality, sodomy, buggery, birth control, atheism, socialism, communism, or any other 'ism. But he may not watch or listen to any critical discussion of the cost, functions, or future of the monarchy. It is assumed, even by critics like Kingsley Martin, that republicanism in Britain is not an immediate political issue, and that the vast majority of the British people would go to the stake in defence of the monarchy.

A book published in 1966 (*Long to Reign Over Us? The Status of the Royal Family in the '60s*, by Leonard M. Harris), gave the results of two surveys carried out by Mass Observation Ltd., on attitudes to the monarchy. They showed that the most fanatical devotee, the unquestioning disciple of the monarchy is the upper class, Tory, regular-Church-of-England-going old lady. At the other extreme – the 'entirely unfavourable' – was the young man in the sixteen to twenty-four age group, with no defined religious views, working class, unskilled, and probably of Communist or other left-fringe political persuasion. The longer in the tooth, the higher in the social scale, the more right wing in politics, the more royalist you are.

But even among declared Tories, only three in every four

were 'wholly favourable' to the monarchy. Among Labour sympathizers, only two out of every four. And contrary to what Kingsley Martin assumes, those with republican views are not as thin on the ground as might be supposed. Mr Harris's surveys show that no less than 36 per cent of the men in the sixteen to forty-five age group, among the skilled working class and those on the left in politics are 'entirely favourable' to the idea of a republic, and 16 per cent said they would actually vote for a republic. Moreover, a substantial majority overall believed that a republic would be more progressive and forward looking. This view was particularly strongly held among people who described themselves as lower middle class. Among the 350 or so Labour MPs in the House of Commons today, I would estimate that at least fifty of them hold republican views. That is far from saying that the rest are ardently and uncritically royalist. Like the vast majority of the British people, I suspect, they give the crown a tacit acceptance rather than enthusiastic and active support. The acceptance is tinged with a compound of indifference, amusement, and ridicule – an attitude similar to that on the only other constitutional institution based on the hereditary principle – the House of Lords. As Mr Harris puts it, the monarchy is 'politically inoffensive', it is an 'effective antidote to party politics' which 'appeal to the lowest instincts of man'.

Not everyone feels so tolerant or kindly towards either the monarchy or the House of Lords. Both institutions reek of aristocratic, hereditary reaction. And just as the attempt has been made to breathe new life into the Lords by the introduction of life peers, so is Prince Philip – no doubt with his ear close to the ground – talking loudly about the need to modernize the monarchy. That the struggle for monarchical survival must be fought in this arena is clearly seen by the one man who has the largest vested interest in survival. This he made clear at a press conference in Canberra on March 2, 1967: 'No one wants to end up like the brontosaurus, who couldn't adapt himself, and who ended up stuffed in a museum . . . it isn't exactly where I want to end up.' On the same occasion, Prince Philip talked about the monarchy as something which 'brings the Commonwealth together'.

As to the first point, the Prince's words have not been matched by deeds in the last fifteen years whilst he has been at the controls.

True, the presentation of debutantes has gone – but hardly any-thing else has changed so that one would notice. The sycophantic press does its best to convince us that things are astir, that the Palace and the court are really 'with it'. For instance, the London *Evening News* carried this gem of an editorial on March 7, 1967:

'Possibly the proudest little girl in London today was Julie Russell, aged nine, who stood with her mother and elder sister in the splendour of the throne room in Buckingham Palace to watch her father receive from the Queen an MBE.

'Julie was there because – being the only member of her family who did not receive an invitation to the investiture – she wrote to the Queen to say: "I am very proud of my daddy and I do want to see you give him the medal."

'Swiftly the rules of protocol were by-passed and a third ticket was on its way to Julie.

'A small thing, but indicative of those changes to which Prince Philip referred the other day – changes which have saved the monarchy from "ending up like a brontosaurus, stuffed in a museum" . . . changes which have bridged the old gulf between royalty and the people and brought a new warmth to their relationship.'

So now we know. The Palace revolution is with us. The excite-ment is killing.

Of course, everybody knows what balderdash that is. The court remains what it has always been – a solid, stuffy, unimaginative Conservative enclave, thick with old Etonians, city men, ex-guards officers, dukes and duchesses, countesses, ladies of the bedchamber, women of the bedchamber, clerks of the closet, and royal peculiars; a strange baggage with which to march fearlessly towards the white heat of the late-twentieth century of techno-logical and scientific revolution. As Prince Philip once inelegantly said: 'It's time we got our finger out'. That particular physical feat should start at the west end of The Mall.

So far as the Commonwealth is concerned, to assume that it is held together by the monarchy is a massive self-deception. It is hardly a less gross delusion to suppose that it will hold together at all over the next twenty years. Australia and New Zealand increasingly look to the United States for defence. They send troops to Vietnam, to help the USA, but not to Hong Kong or Singapore to help the UK. They look more and more to the USA for their capital investment, and to markets other than the UK for their exports. A British entry into the European economic community must further loosen Commonwealth ties. In this context, the monarchy has about as much influence as a parish councillor.

On April 5, 1967, *The Times* carried an article by Hilary Brigstocke, datelined Ottawa April 4, with the headline 'Monarchy as a Divisive Force in the Old Dominions'. This is what it said: 'Much more now is heard about the cult of republicanism and the future of the monarchy in this country. It is being discussed openly – so much so that only a few days ago the *Toronto Daily Star*, a liberal newspaper, had a leading article headed: "Monarchy divides us. A Republic would help Canada." The editorial said flatly: "We believe that the monarchy no longer serves any useful purpose in the task of nation building that lies ahead." ' *The Times* article went on: 'Today there is mostly indifference towards the monarchy except among the older generations of British stock.

'Younger people are either disinterested in the monarchy and its representatives or downright hostile towards it and them ... The younger generations want something new, for they find, as indeed their elders are beginning to discover, that the ceremonial trappings surrounding the upper House of Parliament, the speech from the throne, and the protocol of Government House, are dull and tedious and relics of another age ... The mood of the people here, and, indeed, the mood of the other white dominions, is changing rapidly. Traditional ties with the mother country are becoming much more tenuous.'

For weeks after the death of General George Vanier, the late Governor-General of Canada, the *Toronto Daily Star* ran a campaign for Canada to move to a republic. According to a report in the *Guardian*, on April 21st last, 'The *Star*'s main arguments for a republic have been that one of Canada's failings is a tendency "to imitate rather than innovate" and clinging to this British connection both stultified initiative and made non-British immigrants to Canada feel outsiders.'

As a journalist was overheard to say after Prince Philip's Canberra press conference, it is all a 'bloody bore'. It is even more so to parts of the coloured Commonwealth. The 'link' of monarchy means little or nothing to India, Ghana, Nigeria, Sierra Leone, Zambia, Tanzania, Singapore, Pakistan. Nothing of their future depends on the tinsel and trappings of monarchy. Besotted Labour ministers tried to call in aid the Queen's name to quell rebellion in Rhodesia. Diehard Tories in Britain, and fascist-minded men in Rhodesia, merely yawned or laughed.

I am inclined to agree with Mr Geoffrey Bocca (*The Uneasy Heads*, Weidenfeld and Nicolson, 1959): 'What we live with today is a Cheshire cat monarchy, consisting of a bright smile surrounded by nothing, a frightened, timorous monarchy, hoping not to be noticed so that the death sentence may be delayed.'

It is a harsh judgement. But all over the world, royalty has for long been a dying industry. Redundancy has been high. Existing dynasties are shaking – in Belgium, in Greece, in Holland, and even in Sweden, where republicanism is beginning to flex its muscles.

In Britain the preservationists believe the key to reprieve lies in reform. That is the magic formula, the thing that will at least halt the slow process of ossification and decay. But whatever the future may hold – and the reformers speak with many voices – it is difficult to believe that in a century in which old institutions based on heredity, ancient rituals and meaningless pomp, are being challenged as irrelevant and even dangerous appendages to the body politic, the monarchy, however tarted up, can survive beyond the end of the present reign.

'It becomes a throned monarch better than the crown. . . .'

A. P. HERBERT

Sir Alan Herbert was born in 1890, and was educated at Winchester College and New College, Oxford, where he took a first-class degree in the Honours School of Jurisprudence. He served with the Royal Naval Division in Gallipoli and France, from 1914 to 1917. He was called to the Bar in 1918 and was, for two years, private secretary to Sir Leslie Scott, KC, MP. From 1935 to 1950 he was Independent Member of Parliament for Oxford University In the last war he served with the River Emergency Service (Thames) London, and as a Petty Officer in the Royal Naval Auxiliary Patrol. He has been writing for *Punch* since 1910 and has sat at the famous Table since 1924. He has been a member of the Thames Conservancy Board since 1940. In 1967 he was elected President of the Society of Authors.

PUBLICATIONS
The Secret Battle, The Water Gipsies, Holy Deadlock, Uncommon Law, Independent Member, Number Nine, Why Waterloo?, Made for Man, Bardot MP, The Thames, Sundials Old and New, The Singing Swan, and many volumes of light verse. He was also the author of the libretti of *La Vie Parisienne, Tantivy Towers, Derby Day, Helen, Mother of Pearl, Big Ben, Bless the Bride, Tough at the Top, The Water Gipsies,* and other musical productions, in eight of which he worked with Sir Charles Cochran.

'IF I WERE KING . . .'

A. P. HERBERT

There are some, I believe, who mutter that the monarchy is a lot
of nonsense. I think it is a good example of the English practical
genius in public affairs. The mutterers, the abolishers, never
seem to consider what they are going to put in its place. Every
dunghill must have a senior cock, and however democratic we
become, if every child has one vote, and every 'student' two,
somebody must be head of the state. Somebody must sign
decrees, orders, Acts of Parliament: somebody must represent
the nation on high occasions abroad, in a way that no prime
minister can; somebody must give the medals, launch the ships,
open the universities. Nearly always 'somebody' is a pretty dull
man called the president. But his selection may be far from dull.
There are rivalries, intrigues, partisan manoeuvres, perhaps
elections. At all events there is fuss and fuming: and as a result,
to keep everyone happy, perhaps the last man that anybody wants
is chosen. He may not have wanted the job himself, or have any
particular aptitude for it. Thus, because of the invincible
jealousies of Melbourne and Sydney, our dear Australia finished
up with a capital at Canberra. The United States, it is true,
have a Vice-President ready, but he has generally been selected
for the same sort of reason as Canberra.

But look how the British manage these affairs. 'The King is
dead – Long live the King!' is the most practical saying in history.
There is no fuss, no argument about their new head of state.
He is there, on the spot, fit and ready. If it were considered
seemly he could lay a foundation stone, plant a tree, or open a
parliament, with the authority of the nation, the very next day.
No party has cause to complain, no disappointed statesman
weeps in his bath. Moreover, the new head has been trained
for the job (not an easy one) ever since he threw his first toy
out of his pram or used a cross word in the nursery: and if the
new head dies untimely or abdicates there are more good colts
ready in the same efficient stable.

Even some of the mystical stuff about the monarchy has, or may have, a practical significance. All our statutes, as I hope they teach the schoolboys still, are passed by 'the Queen in Parliament'. At the head of each Act are these words:

'Be it enacted therefore by the Queen's most Excellent Majesty, by and with the advice and consent of the Lords Spiritual and Temporal, and Commons in this present Parliament assembled, and by the authority of the same, as follows:'

It is rather like the Trinity: 'And yet they are not three legislative bodies but one legislative body.' The Queen plays a modest part, like the Holy Ghost. In theory she is 'assembled' too, she is present in Parliament all the time, though in fact she would be requested to leave if she was. Things were even said, in 1846, when Albert, the royal spouse, heard a debate from the press gallery of the House of Commons: and he did not attend again.

The Queen does, though, open Parliament in person, and summons the Commons to the Lords to hear the gracious speech from the throne which indicates what 'my ministers' propose to do. At the end of the session she gives the Royal Assent to all the Bills the other two legislators have passed, and signs them. It is not till then that they become *Acts* of Parliament. She used to give the Royal Assent present in person, and I have often wished that the monarch would do that now, not only to compliment Lords and Commons on their labours, but to make the ancient partnership of Crown with Lords and Commons in the making of laws physically manifest.

The Queen still signifies her will in the ancient Norman French formulae. If she assents she says (or, in her absence, the Lords Commissioners say it for her): '*La Reine le veult.*' If it is a money Bill she says: '*La Reine remercie ses bons sujets, accepte leur benevolence, et ainsi le veult.*' The third formula is: '*La Reine s'avisera.*'

It is surprising, by the way, that no modern monarch has declined to use these foreign formulae, which must remind us of the only conquest of England. There is a precedent for protest. During the Commonwealth the Lord Protector insisted on giving his assent in English. In 1786 the House of Lords passed a Bill for abolishing the use of the French tongue in all proceedings in Parliament: but in the Commons – more conservative? – it was dropped. But I do not myself see why legislation should be necessary. She has to say the words, not Parliament. So long as she does not interfere with matters of policy she can, I imagine, correct a grammatical error or pompous infelicity in the Gracious Speech submitted by 'My Ministers'. I hope she does. Why should she not, like Cromwell, insist upon speaking the Queen's English when she gives birth to a statute?

No monarch has said '*La Reine s'avisera*' since 1707 when Queen Anne refused her assent to a Bill for settling the militia in Scotland.

Every man at Westminster would swear that those words will never be heard again: for 'the prerogative is dead'. But wait a minute. On this subject I have had some jolly constitutional dreams. Suppose the House of Commons went mad and voted itself salaries of £10,000 a year for each member with tax free expenses of £5,000. The House of Lords could not touch it, for it would be a 'Money Bill', and they were warned off such measures by the Parliament Act. Suppose that Her Majesty came down to the House, and when this Bill was laid before her she said firmly: '*La Reine s'avisera.*' Nothing but brute force could stop her. It would be one of the most popular acts in British history. The statesmen might yell: 'The royal prerogative is dead.' The people would yell back: 'It seems to be alive – and a good thing too.'

I had an even jollier dream, which I developed as a 'misleading case' in *Punch* (November 30, 1966). The Air (Nationalization) Bill, just before the summer 'recess', was hurried through both Houses. Its purpose was social justice – and more taxation. Air, said the ministers, was inequitably distributed and enjoyed. The castles, mansions, and flats of the rich occupied more air than the humble dwellings of the poor. Top flats got more air than the ground floor, fat men occupied more air than the thin, bachelors than families, and so on. Everyone, and everything, was to be measured, and at the end there would be just taxation on every (estimated) ounce of air the citizen drew and every inch of air he and his dwelling displaced.

In both Houses there had recently been increasing complaints about the unnecessary unintelligibility of some of the Bills put before them. There was even an ugly suggestion that the obscurity was sometimes deliberately created in order that the Treasury or other department might whip in a few monstrous deeds before the citizen and his solicitor knew where they were.

On the Air (N) Bill there were the usual protests. One Minister, having duly delivered a speech supplied by Whitehall about the administrative arrangements, confessed that he was far from understanding all of it.

But both Lords and Commons (and their wives) were thinking of the summer holidays and did not want to shorten them for 'a mere matter of words'. The Commons were half dead with all-night sittings already, and did not want any more. A mass of amendments was put down by the Law Lords, who would have to interpret the Bill later on, and they were duly discussed: but none of them was sent to the Commons. It looked as if Whitehall had won another sneaky and shameful success.

But the Queen's most Excellent Majesty had read, and heard, about this Bill. She sent for the Minister in charge and asked him to explain Paragraph 5 of Schedule 4 and other passages. The answers, it seems, were not considered satisfactory. Also, the story went, she had something to say about the barbarous practice known as 'legislation by reference'. The Interpretation clause, for example, said:

'In this Act the expression "Air" has the meaning attributed to it in Sub-section 7 of Section 14 of the Land Drainage Act 1930, except in Section 5 and 119 of this Act where it shall be interpreted in like manner as the same expression in Section 85 of the Civil Aviation Act 1923.'

'How are the judges,' said the Queen, 'how is anyone, to understand that?'

'Counsel or clerks, Ma'am, seek out the necessary statutes and lay them before the judge.'

'But what about the ordinary man – or indeed the Queen? So far as I know, there is no copy of the Land Drainage Act 1930 in this Palace – or even the Civil Aviation Act 1923. I have not the slightest idea what is meant by the word "Air" in the Air (Nationalization) Bill to which I am asked to give my assent. And you, Sir, are unable to tell me.'

Altering her own holiday arrangements the Queen gave notice

that on July 31st when a batch of Bills was coming up for Assent she would attend the House of Lords in person. She took her place on the throne. Black Rod summoned the faithful Commons, some of whom, led by the Speaker, the Prime Minister and Leader of the Opposition behind him, crowded into the small space at the Bar.

The Clerk of the Parliaments read the names of nine Bills, and to each Her Majesty replied:

'*La Reine le veult.*'

Then came Number 10: Air (Nationalization) Bill.

Her Majesty replied, to the general astonishment: '*La Reine s'avisera,*' but she added words which were new to all: '*La Reine ne comprend pas ceste bille.*'

There was a respectful hush till the Queen departed: but the faithful Commons walked back to their chamber noisily protesting. The Prime Minister and his followers took the severe view that Her Majesty had rejected the Bill and that this was an unconstitutional exercise of a defunct prerogative. The silliest among them wanted a savage General Election at once. But the more thoughtful observed that the Queen had not in terms rejected the Bill. She had not said: '*La Reine ne le veult pas*' but '*La Reine s'avisera*'. This, for a long time, had been taken as tantamount to a rejection; but was that necessary? The Queen was using the ancient words in their literal meaning. She needed time to consult and consider, for the simple reason that, as presented to her, the Bill was unintelligible. She did not, the civil servants said, 'exclude the possibility' that if the same Bill were presented to her in reasonably lucid form she would be able to say: '*La Reine le veult.*' She clearly thought, though she had not publicly said so, that her two partners had done an inferior job, and she did not want to put her name to it without a protest.

When this point became clear to the people there was a surge of popular approval for the Queen's action, for few of the citizens had not suffered at one time or another from unintelligible laws or dubious regulations. There was no more talk of a General Election. Instead the Prime Minister, very sensibly, referred the constitutional point as a special question to the Judicial Committee of the Privy Council, under Section 4 of the Act of 1833.

The Judicial Committee, through a former Lord Chancellor, said:

'Few Acts of Parliament can be instantly intelligible to the ordinary citizen – that would be too much to expect; but my learned brothers and I, accustomed for decades to the painful study of such documents, are agreed that for complexity and cloud this one takes all prizes . . . We are now asked to determine whether Her Majesty's action can be described as unconstitutional, whether, that is, she has exercised a power which was once part of the royal prerogative (strange expression) but is no more. First, let me say that an ancient constitutional phrase must not be presumed to have lost all force because it has not been used for a long time. *"The King can do no wrong"* does not mean so much as it did, in that a minister or government department can now be sued by a citizen: but it still means much, and its partial diminution had to be effected by an Act of Parliament. There has never been a formal exclusion of the phrase *"La Reine s'avisera"* from the vocabulary of the Constitution, so we conclude that in proper circumstances it may still be employed. If there was any evidence that Her Majesty had rejected, or even delayed, the Bill because of its principle or purpose, that is, because she was personally opposed to the nationalization of the air, we might have to express an embarrassing opinion. Fortunately, there is no such evidence, and we find nothing unconstitutional in her gracious behaviour. The Queen has acted as one of the three partners in the business of law-making, and she has acted in the cause of efficiency, nothing else. "The Lords Spiritual and Temporal" and "the Commons in this present Parliament assembled" may be content to let something called a "law" go forth in this form, knowing that by its exotic language and obscure intent it is bound to cause injustice among the citizens and endless exertion and expense in the courts of law. The Queen, more conscientious than her partners, has simply said: "I will not put my name to this foggy and deceiving document. Nationalize the Air, by all means, but do it in terms which can be understood by my educated subjects." '

One of the virtues of the loose arrangements called the British constitution is its capacity to bud and flourish in unexpected places. It is comforting to those of us who interpret the laws to find that in the nick of time a new fertilizer for clarity has been disclosed. Henceforth every legislator, every parliamentary draftsman, will bear in mind the thought that, if he is not careful, at the end of his labours the Queen may say: '*La Reine s'avisera.*'

'We hope she will not hesitate to say it again.'

My fairy tale may have a sound foundation. Friends of the monarchy are always afraid of the monarch, or her spouse, doing too much and thus incurring the displeasure of the sour. I think, so long as they do not impinge on 'politics', the more they do the better – though it is difficult now, I agree, to touch anything that may not have a touch of the political tarbrush. In anything non-political, anything where they may be considered to have a personal mind or taste the Royals should hold themselves free to exercise it, without having to consult 'my ministers'. Their impact on our games and pleasures is splendid – the Queen at Ascot, or the Cup Final, or Lord's, Princess Marina at Wimbledon, Princess Margaret at the play, the Duke's sailing and polo, his youth awards and his sorties into science. (He was, by the way, the final mover of the *Cutty Sark* into her honourable bed at Greenwich, and was active in the affair long before that.)

I wish there were more to tell. For example, in a paragraph which irritated me I read: ' "The appointment of a Poet Laureate to succeed Mr John Masefield ... will not be for some time," *a spokesman for the Prime Minister* said yesterday.' Excuse me, but what has this got to do with Mr Wilson? The Poet Laureate is one of Her Majesty's Household, one of that glorious little roll you may see in Whitaker's Almanack:

Master of the Music	Sir Arthur Bliss
Poet Laureate	John Edward Masefield
Bargemaster	H. A. Barry
Keeper of the Swans	F. J. Turk

The Queen should surely be able to say to Mr Wilson: 'I want John Betjeman for my Poet Laureate' (if she does). 'I've talked him into it, and I shall appoint him today. What is more, I'm making it a three-year appointment, so that I can give others a chance. The next will be Mr – – .'

I wish there were Queen's Prizes for books and plays awarded by the Queen herself. Her choices might not be those of Sloane Square or Soho, but they might set a salutary fashion. How splendid if Sir Francis Chichester had been financed by Her Majesty and the Duke together! It would have been the bet of her life. How grand a thing if they turned up on the last night of the Proms!

There is precedent for that. I was privileged to be present at that thrilling concert at the opening of the Royal Festival Hall. The King (George VI) and Queen were in the box, and I *think*, the present Queen. Sir Malcolm Sargent had got hold of Arne's original manuscript of *Rule Britannia*. In this the famous refrain, which, sung by most of us, sounds like a funeral dirge, was found to be full of dotted notes and, played by Sir Malcolm, sounded like a gay piece from a 'musical', which is what it was. (It comes from a masque called *Alfred,* and was sung, in the finale, I believe, by King Alfred. The first performance was given in 1740 at Cliveden, then the residence of the Prince of Wales, to celebrate his birthday.) Sir Malcolm had also discovered some swift, exciting trumpet passages before, during, and after each verse. He had a huge choir and, high above them, I do not know how many trumpeters in costume. We all went mad. We insisted on encores. Aneurin Bevan, at the other end of my row, was clapping like a good Conservative Englishman. A great night.

The next time they met, the King said to Sir Malcom: 'I loved your *Rule Britannia* that night. Whenever I come to one of your concerts you must play it again – just like that.'

'I like it too, Sir – but it might not always be suitable.'

'Not suitable? *Rule Britannia?* What d'you mean?' said King George VI.

'Well, Sir, I might be playing the *Matthew Passion.*'

'That's all right,' said His Majesty, 'I shouldn't be there.'[1]

The tale does not, you may think, put King George VI very high among musical critics: but the point is, he would have loved the last night of the Proms, and one visit to any Prom would have put that great British musical institution even higher than it is.

We must never turn up our noses at royal pleasures: for if you look about our little land you will see that nearly always they gave us space and beauty – lasting beauty – and sometimes more, the royal dwellings – Windsor, Hampton Court, Sion House, Westminster, Somerset House, above all Greenwich, the brightest gem in Greater London. Here, as I have said before, is

---

[1] This is not confidence-breaking. Sir Malcolm kept the story private for many years: but we extracted it from him in his seventieth birthday broadcast on B.B.C. Television.

monarchy's most grand advertisement. Cross the river to the north side, to the Isle of Dogs, and look through the gap between the wings of the Palace – now the Royal Naval College – up the green hill to Flamsteed's old observatory at the top. You will see what I have called the prime pearl of the tideway. A better man has spoken of 'the most stately procession of buildings we possess ... one of the most sublime sights English architecture affords.' Someone else named it 'the widest panorama in London'. Yet everything you see we owe not to the wisdom of state planners, but to the work, sometimes the whims, of Kings and Queens. They are everywhere in the Greenwich story, and everywhere they left behind them not only beauty but benefit. Duke Humphrey, brother of Henry V, and Regent after his death, built a country house where the College stands today. But says Mr Frank Carr, in an excellent little book,[1] he made it a centre of learning for scholars and artists. We owe the park to his poor nephew, Henry VI. It was the first of the royal parks. His wife (but she was a wild French girl) turned the 'centre of learning', Bella Court, into a palace of pleasaunce, or *placentia*. Henry VIII hunted and hawked in the park (and there are deer in the park today) but as well he watched the King's ships in the fine dockyard he had built at Deptford. James I built a high brick wall about the park and that still stands. Charles II, in 1675, 'resolved to build a small observatory within our Park at Greenwich, upon the highest ground': he appointed Flamsteed, the first Astronomer Royal, and this in the end made Greenwich the centre of the world for seamen and astronomers. (In the old observatory and Flamsteed's house you can now see the whole history charmingly displayed.)

But King William III (William of Orange), or rather his queen, the well-loved Mary of York, provide the best story of royal creation, for it concerns the whole scene. Some way back from the college is the beautiful Queen's House, the home today of the National Maritime Museum. This was planned by Inigo Jones in 1616 for the wife of James I, and was completed by Charles I for his own. It had a clear view to the river.

In 1692, after the great naval victory of La Hogue, the Palace decided to use the King's House on the bank at Greenwich as a

---

[1] *Maritime Greenwich* (1965)—A Pitkin 'Pride of Britain' book.

F

Seamen's Hospital, to match Chelsea's hospital for soldiers. The great Sir Christopher Wren was summoned. He wanted, it seems, to pull down the King's House, and the Queen's House too, and start again – one grand edifice with a majestic dome in the middle. But Mary said no. There should be a second wing on the east side to balance the King's House, and between them there was to be a gap 115 feet wide. *The Queen's House must keep its view.*

Thus Wren dutifully built not one dome but two, which look to me like two daughters of St Paul's. One is over the chapel, the other over the famous Painted Hall, both magnificent. 'Royal selfishness again' the sour may say: but see the result. From the river, or from the Isle of Dogs on the opposite shore you can see not only the two splendid wings of the palace, but, through Queen Mary's 'gap', first, the Queen's House, which, in its modest way, is as beautiful, and holds today, in the museum, the whole long story of Britain's achievements on the sea and in the sky. Then, beyond the Queen's House, you can see the steep hill of the park and at the top the old observatory which has played so great a part in the affairs of the world. Mr Frank Carr has called it 'the most unaltered view' and indeed it is just as Canaletto painted it in 1755. How fortunate that, centuries ago, the kings and queens chose Greenwich as a place of pleasure and saved it from the planners and the local authorities! What a pity that some king did not make a mansion and a park on the river bank below St Paul's!

I wish the Queen and Prince Philip (why on earth is he not Prince Consort?) could make such a contribution to the London scene today. They cannot love, any more than you and I do, the proliferating topless towers which stick up like vertical weeds all over London. If only they were tapered, and topped with the graceful spires and turrets which make the New York 'skyline' the wonder of the world there would be some hope for London's. I cannot believe that architecture is responsible for all these horrors: it must be commerce and economy. I wish the Queen would buy some 'development area' and put up some graceful buildings – even if they were but flats or offices – which would be a model to the land. I dare say a bank or two would lend her the money.

Then, if I were the monarch I should ask the state to talk less about 'the Crown' in unpleasant or unpopular contexts, in which what is really meant is 'the state'. The Bill of Rights, 1689, has much to say about 'The Crown and Government of this Realm'. Every person who 'shall profess the Popish religion ... shall be excluded, and be for ever incapable to inherit, possess, or enjoy the Crown and Government of this Realm ...' Such language was well enough when the monarch did play a large part in government. But now, shorn of most of my powers, I should like the word 'Crown' to mean me personally and not the often detestable state. Queen Victoria, in her early days, used to sign with her own hand the warrants for the execution of condemned criminals: but she soon transferred this unpleasant duty to the Home Secretary. That was a good precedent. It is 'the Crown', not the Queen, that demands the subject's money from Parliament, and smells their breath, and does many other odious things. The citizen should not be warned off 'crown property' unless it is in some way personal and private to the Queen: a dockyard or a nuclear establishment should be 'state' property. Passports are still issued 'in the name of Her Majesty'. Since they are now nothing but costly nuisances, I should insist on having my name taken off them. I am not sure that I should want to be the prosecution in every criminal case – *Regina v. Haddock*. Is there not here, by the way, a constitutional oddity? The Queen, as the fount of justice, is supposed to be present in all her courts as she is in Parliament. To this day, I believe, when she enters the City of London any of her judges at work, at the Old Bailey for example, adjourn the cases they are considering until she withdraws from the City. For who are they to administer the Queen's justice when the Queen herself is at hand, and – who knows? – may wish to appear on her Bench in person. This is a delightful fancy which I would not abolish. But then, if she is to try the case of *Regina v. Haddock* she is surely both prosecution and judge, she is trying her own case, which is contrary to natural justice and the high principles of Britain. The lawyers, no doubt, have some cunning answer to this: but I should still (if monarch) object to being made a party to every petty larceny or drunk-while-driving case. Let it be *The State v. Haddock*.

I should have a firm word too with my Prime Minister, or perhaps, my Lord Chancellor, about 'the Prerogative of Mercy' and the whole 'pardon' department. The great Blackstone said that the power of pardoning offences was one of the great advantages of monarchy in general above every other form of government, and 'cannot subsist in democracies'. It does subsist in this one for it is exercised in fact by the Home Secretary, though he is supposed to be 'advising' Her Majesty. But many simple citizens suppose that when the royal prerogative is mercifully employed the Queen makes a personal decision, and distracted wives write to her in person. Perhaps no great harm is done here, but I feel that in such a case, if ever I differed from my Home Secretary, my verdict should be allowed to prevail.

Certainly I would have nothing to do with the absurd business of granting 'a free pardon' to a man who is found to have been wrongfully convicted and may even have served a sentence of imprisonment, like Adolf Beck. Far back in 1848 Lord Chief Justice Denman and two other judges protested against this anomaly before a Select Committee of the House of Lords. Another protest was made by the Beck Commission in 1904. In 1907 Parliament sought to end it by Section 4 of the Criminal Appeal Act, which provided that the Court of Criminal Appeal might quash a conviction and direct a judgement and verdict of acquittal be entered. But this course is not always convenient; for one thing, it means that the case must come up in court again: and from time to time an innocent man is still graciously accorded a royal 'free pardon'. 'If I were king' I should hotly refuse to put my hand to so nonsensical a document. I would sign a decree of innocence and royal regret, but not a 'free pardon' to someone who had done no wrong.

The pursuit and capture by the newspapers of 'personality' tales and pictures in the royal circle may often seem to be overdone. But it represents a real interest among the common people. We recognize that the Queen and Prince Philip are mortals like ourselves, but we feel in our hearts that they are somehow different from us, superior to all of us, in a way that Mr Wilson and Mr Heath are not. It is, I think, a wholesome, almost a spiritual feeling, like the agnostic's grudging admission that somewhere there is some kind of a god. High and low feel better when they have seen the Queen, more resolute and ready for duty, as some of us do when we hear the royal anthem. The ancient pageantry, the gracious customs and disciplines, reinforce the feeling. I was privileged to see the Queen lay that sword on Sir Francis Chichester's shoulder in the great courtyard at Greenwich. The choice of scene was a stroke of genius. The occasion would not have been quite the same if President Wilson had pinned a medal on the hero's breast and given him a certificate of knighthood. And would it have been at Greenwich?

Our women cannot wait to hear what the Queen was wearing. They would give a lot to hear what she is saying to the Duke of Norfolk in the paddock. The men admire and envy Prince Philip's feats on the water, on horseback, in the air. We all, I think, enjoy his sage, straight speeches. We should like to hear more of the Queen's opinions on non-political affairs. What does she think about the latest buildings, about cigarette smoking, pop songs, 'summer time', the new starting stalls, modern poetry, modern dancing, even mini-skirts? I do not want to see her shopping on a bicycle, like some monarchs abroad. But anything that makes us feel that for all her dignity and distance she is 'one of us' must be good. The Christmas broadcast is a fine example: but all through the year she must sometimes wish that she could break away from the dull words given to her – and why should she not? Erskine May said somewhere: 'The Queen cannot be supposed to have a private opinion apart from that of her responsible advisers.' To that, if I were king, I would say: 'With certain limits, Prime Minister, Tosh! You statesmen have removed my power, but you are not going to take my personality too. I must, I know, be a political figurehead: but a personal figurehead, no. For example, you may bring up your Permanent Summer Time Bill, and I shall have to give it my royal assent: but the clocks in this Palace will tell Greenwich mean time in the winter.'

GEORGE HIGGINS

George Higgins was born in 1916 in Neuilly-sur-Seine in France. His father was a French banker. He studied in Switzerland and took a degree in literature at the Sorbonne. During the war he worked for the French resistance helping Allied pilots escape from occupied territory.

He is a journalist and has been editor of *Paris-Match*. He is now editor of *France-Dimanche*, a popular French weekly with a circulation of one and a half million.

MONARCHIE A L'ANGLAISE

G. W. HIGGINS

The future of the British monarchy? Only an uninformed or presumptuous man can reply to this question without a smile, or a pang.

The future, as every thinking and feeling person is well aware, 'belongs to no man'. But it is not forbidden us to speculate and to say, basing ourselves on the existing situation, 'this, in my view, is what is going to happen' – especially as we have the good fortune to be able to draw upon a fairly broad field of experience.

Nevertheless, we must realize the futility of our enterprise. The future lies at the mercy of some discovery, some sudden mutation, which no logic could foresee. Five years ago it seemed that road and air travel would supersede the train, but today the hovertrain has again laid this open to question. Who could have predicted the recovery of the Catholic Church after the papal cowardice of the war, and the revolutionary tide which swept over central Europe? The future is at the mercy of a nation's driving spirit, and it is one of the glories of man that he continually outstrips his reason and his thought. If the prophets are sometimes proved right, they owe it to the god of chance. This I sincerely believe.

As the editor of a popular newspaper with a very wide circulation, I am in a position to assess the appeal of the various members of the British Royal Family in the countries of Europe, and judge their impact.

As regards England, our judgements will be, by contrast, theoretical and bookish, and no doubt the reader will find them far less interesting. But this too is an aspect of our subject, and we shall deal with it briefly, on the supposition that the views of a journalist from outside can have some value, coming from afar.

The future of the monarchy in England seems assured. Who or what constitutes a threat to it? Nothing, apparently, and nobody. What about communism? This hypothesis is self-destructive. A republic, then? Events past and present in various European countries amply prove to the subjects of Her Most Gracious Majesty that a republic offers fewer guarantees of freedom and individual well-being than the monarchy in the form in which it exists in England. As a journalist, I do not find the young people of England anti-royalist, and nothing could have seemed more natural than to see Queen Elizabeth bountifully rewarding the shaggy Beatles and Mary Quant, inventor of the mini-skirt.

Nowhere in England does one sense an anti-monarchist under-current. There are isolated gestures, but these have no deep significance. This peaceful state of affairs can be explained, I think, by the fact that the monarchy does not set itself against social reform or economic change. It takes no active part in the class struggle. Therein lies its strength and, may I add, its greatness.

I see no reason why every Englishman, albeit poor, needy or out of work, should not sing today 'God save our Gracious Queen' (in France on the other hand, he might find it hard to shout 'Vive de Gaulle!').

If there were a threat, it could only come from the direction of the continent. The great economic fusion which must take place, and in which Great Britain is bound to be involved, will inevitably be accompanied by a compounding of ideas and ideals, and it is conceivable that the British throne might totter beneath the combined pressures of the republican peoples of Europe. But I do not think, speaking from experience, that this is a real danger.

To understand this and convince ourselves of it, we only have to observe the measure of popularity which the figures of British royalty enjoy, and the lively interest taken in them by the good people of France or Belgium, Switzerland, Italy and others. We all know how an idea dies out if the man who embodies it is hated, and how, inversely, it will prosper and bear fruit if the person or persons who represent it stir the hearts of the multitude. No revolution can take place without hatred, no triumph is won without love.

On the continent the Queen enjoys wild and dazzling success. In France, Germany and Italy the mere fact that her photograph appears on the front of a newspaper or magazine virtually ensures its success. *France-Dimanche, Jours de France, Paris-Match,*

Stop, Oggi, Stern, are the living proof of this. On the continent, if a popular magazine reaches a low in circulation and its head of sales is interrogated about the best way to stop a further falling off, it is odds on that the confident reply will come: 'Elizabeth'.

This is not hearsay – I myself have been subjected to fierce pressure of this kind. Urged by my sales manager, whose brilliance is equalled only by his temper, I had the effrontery to figure Queen Elizabeth on the front page of seven successive issues of *France-Dimanche,* which, according to all the specialists of the art, was sheer suicide. But, my paper gained readers with each issue. Of course, there was topical interest, and my editorial staff displayed no little skill, but this successs must be attributed, above all, to the Queen's mythical powers of attraction for a non-British public.

I am sure that all editing annals are full of stories of this kind. I myself could furnish numerous examples, but none could be more eloquent in its arithmetical and repetitive simplicity than the one I have just cited.

In Berlin, Rome or Brussels the Queen attracts more attention than any other head of state, at home or visiting there. In Paris itself, she would draw more crowds than General de Gaulle, who has such a mystic fascination for the French. Yes, let our Elizabeth make her progress down the Champs Elysées, and the throng would be even greater than the crowds which would turn out to see the implacable, solitary and ageing figure to whom France owes her resurrection and salvation.

The most comforting thing about this adultation of the masses – from the point of view of the future of the British monarchy – is that it is prompted, not only by the Queen, and the way she performs her Queenly task, but equally by the monarchy itself.

After so many shabby and undistinguished republics, Europe is thirsting after glamour and ceremonial uniforms. What more attractive than this gracious monarchy with its impeccable protocol? It holds no sway in politics; it causes its servants to waltz once a year; its manners are far more democratic than those of a certain president of the republic with whom we are closely acquainted.

Viewed from the Continent, the British monarchy appears in a romantic light (countless Europeans have made the journey just to see the Changing of the Guard!). This is where it scores over an unromantic republic. The peoples of Europe find themselves drawn towards Elizabeth, I think, as towards a Hollywood star, but the monarchy has the ingredients of pomp, magnificence and power (at any rate apparent) without the scandalous private life, the occasional sordid incidents and distasteful roles of Hollywood; as a result enthusiasm is deeper and more genuine.

Is it possible to isolate those characteristics of the Queen which make her so popular? This analysis, I think, would not prove uninteresting; it is not perhaps a prime factor in trying to determine the future of the monarchy, but it is nonetheless a piece of documentation of interest to all those who take the future of the Windsors to heart, and moreover points out what one must avoid, if one wishes to retain the admiration and respect of continental crowds.

One of the Queen's greatest assets is her devotion to her task. The tired look on her face, the rumours which speak of exhaustion and fatigue, endear yet further this sovereign who took up the crown under circumstances which fired the public imagination. It was on a voyage with her young and handsome husband, in the romantic seclusion of an exotic hotel surrounded by the wild life of the African forest, that she learned the tragic news of her beloved father's death; although almost a girl as yet, she had to take up the sceptre of an insecure and divided empire, part of which already lay in ruins. Certain ceremonies very aptly illustrate her professionally conscientious attitude. I am thinking especially of Trooping the Colour. To see her sitting stiff and motionless upon her mount for a full hour or more fills the whole of Europe with admiration. What woman, be she French, Italian or German, has not been touched by the weary and desperate way she glances over her shoulder at her husband, as if demanding of him the courage to go through with this procession – so unfeminine, so out of keeping with the aspiration of a young modern woman. On the continent this symbolic image is awaited year by year as an embodiment of the Queen and her devotion to duty. To destroy it by bringing the ceremony up to date would deal a blow to the tourist industry, and to the prestige of the monarchy.

Another quality which wins the Queen an enthusiatic following is her gravity, her austerity. Nothing scandalous or unseemly has ever attached to her name or been bandied about from mouth to mouth. The continental people are so thoroughly persuaded of her deep sense of duty and moral rectitude that the Margaret-Townsend episode only increased her stature. She could have built up resentment by sacrificing her young sister for reasons of state, and with anyone else, this might have been the case; but coming from Elizabeth the act revealed yet another aspect of her greatness.

The reader should not shrug his shoulders here, or accuse us of cheap sentimentality. These are the thoughts and feelings of the European public – the group with which we are concerned. The *élite* groups, who think and feel quite differently, are far from fostering the same attachment for the British monarchy. Quite the opposite, in fact – the French, German and Italian royalists of our acquaintance are frankly hostile to the British monarchy. They accuse it, among other things, of being too democratic, too much at the service of its people.

In France the fierce devotion to Elizabeth springs from the heart of the republican masses, which seems to me to be a most encouraging sign for the future. The French people were the first revolutionaries and regicides of Europe, and if their passion has abated, where else could such sentiments survive?

Let us now examine the feelings of these masses who make the mighty tremble, and assure the success of the popular press – their feelings with regard to the husband of the Queen. Here we are no longer on such simple ground, as feelings undergo a subtle change from year to year.

The young betrothed of the heir to the throne met with a varied reception. If certain people, women especially, extolled his handsome features and noble bearing, others secretly accused him of marrying for money. It must be admitted that circumstances are not in his favour; on the one hand an heiress fabulously endowed, but with no claim to beauty; on the other a prince with the dazzling good looks of a film star, but without a penny to his name. Dear readers, come to your own conclusions . . .

However, when a few years had passed this unflattering image was replaced by a much more endearing one. The penniless lack-land prince gave way to the devoted husband, doing his utmost to support his wife in the prodigious, complex and well-nigh hopeless task for which she seemed so ill prepared. Where the

Queen went, he went too, discrete and attentive, always ready to fly to her rescue with word or gesture. For years the continental press went on publishing the same photograph (in the foreground the Queen, looking slightly stiff, and wearing a forced smile; behind her the prince, radiating confidence and manly charm). Far from growing tired of it, the public lapped it up.

For several years now this heartening political and matrimonial image has been superseded by a third: the emancipated husband. He is still there to bear the brunt, but he is no longer the sovereign's faithful shadow. He has on occasion taken the leading role, and does not hesitate, if the opportunity arises, to take a bold initiative, even if it runs contrary to the strict tradition of royal protocol. He sometimes looks a trifle bored, as if he found the whole thing rather silly. He ducks press men, harangues industrialists, sets off on a voyage round the world and grows his beard, to show that he is a free man.

This is no Prince Charming but a mature man, thinking for himself and living his own life. Some people would go so far as to say that it is he who is the King.

Opinion is divided in consequence, some accusing him of slightly neglecting his wife, of staying away at Christmas and forgetting his children's birthdays. Others, on the contrary, are attracted by his daring, adventurous streak. However this may be, his appearances on continental television awaken men's curiosity, win him friends and set women's hearts a-flutter.

The case of Margaret is equally complex. She undoubtedly excites curiosity. She has a vivid and original personality; she is 'with it', apt to do the unexpected, and loves to create a stir. Nevertheless, contact with my vast reading public of five millions permits me to ascertain that she no longer enjoys the popularity she used to at the time of her unhappy love affair with Townsend. She has destroyed her legend by marrying a playboy photographer. As one of our women readers put it to me last April: 'She expects to have all the advantages of being a princess, as well as the advantages of being an ordinary woman.' This duality in her behaviour, which is very evident from here, is certainly one reason for the falling off of her public. She is thought capricious and unpredictable; she has departed from her prescribed pattern and paid the price.

To this analysis must be added one other factor of considerable importance. For several years now Margaret has had a rival who, after a bad beginning, is now gaining followers every day among the crowds: Princess Paula of Belgium. Her gay and unself-conscious manner, and her refusal to stand upon ceremony, go down extremely well. It is rather curious that a quality which in Margaret fails to please seems to be an asset in Paula's case; this may be because she is a simpler woman, and widely known to be an excellent mother to her children. However, these factors do not provide a complete explanation. It seems to me that they cannot in themselves account for Paula's greater popularity. It may be that young women identify with her because they too feel the urge to break with tradition, to enter the new world of the mini-skirt and the Pill.

Whatever the reasons, the fact remains that Paula is continually gaining ground. Another rival has also played a part in detracting from the prestige of the Queen's younger sister, although she has been less in evidence since Paula came upon the scene: Princess Alexandra. At one time, I think it would be true to say the public over here literally went mad about her. It extended a delighted welcome to this un-Victorian princess, from a rather formal Royal Family, with her boyish looks and ready smile, her complete lack of ceremony and evident enjoyment of a joke. But it must be admitted that after her relatively undistinguished marriage, she has been less in the limelight.

One strongly controversial figure within the Royal Family is Tony, who, according to our knowledge (or more accurately, pretended knowledge) of popular psychology, ought to attract sympathy: not this time the shepherdess marrying a king, but the shepherd marrying the queen, or rather the princess – an archetypal role which has been played out countless times, generating envious sighs, thrilling the female soul and creating secret hopes within the bosoms of our women readers...! Nevertheless, the fact remains that with Tony the alchemy did not take place, and he is not a popular figure. The story of his life leaves the public cold. A devastating example, if you like, is the occasion when the announcement of a possible divorce produced absolutely no effect upon the public, even the veteran grannies' brigade, who weep at every royal birth, and feel themselves to be personally involved in every royal baptism. When this news was featured in the headlines of the biggest French newspaper, the evening daily *France-Soir,* a drop in sales resulted. It matters little that the news was true or false; as journalists well know, it is the *reaction* to its announcement which is important, as it allows us to gauge the receptivity of the public to a certain person or event.

What has Tony done to deserve so much indifference, and indeed hostility? Any explanation must be hypothetical – it is with this reservation that we proffer our own.

Once within the magic circle, Tony should have behaved in the manner required of him by such an exceptional stroke of fate. Cinderella, once the miracle was wrought, conducted herself like a princess; she did not take the rags of her poverty with her into the magic world whither the fairy wand had carried her, but this is exactly what Tony did. The photographer remained a photographer and continued to dress like a Mod.

One small incident shows the course he should have adopted to gain a following among the masses: the news that he had undertaken to design a special chair for severely handicapped polio victims was received with the liveliest interest by my female readers. The good Doctor Jung, who discovered the 'collective unconscious', would have had a lot to say on the subject.

And now here is something which shows how strongly the image of the monarchy imposes itself on the Continent: the 'lame ducks' of the family (if I may be permitted to use this disrespectful expression to designate the non-starters in the popularity stakes like the Duke of Windsor, Princess Margaret and Tony), far from detracting from the Queen's prestige, merely enhance it. She is not measured against them, but they against her, and Elizabeth gains by the comparison every time.

This is the reward for exemplary behaviour, for conducting oneself in all particulars in the manner expected of one.

At this point in our discourse it might perhaps be interesting to examine the influence of the Windsor affair on public opinion – did it or did it not diminish the prestige of the British monarchy in Europe?

For my own part I believe that when this king succumbed like any ordinary man to love and, struck by Cupid's dart, relinquished an Empire, he did a great deal for the popularity of the English Royal Family.

The public said to itself: 'If this king can lose his head over a woman and do a silly thing like that, why, he is one of us.' As for the Royal Family itself, it afforded the public a further opportunity for identifying, by reacting like any family displeased with the matrimonial choice of one of its sons: with anger, with ostracism and with exile.

I think that the public airing of this dramatic episode was an excellent thing for the image of the monarchy. Crowds love to participate in the tragedies which overtake the great ones of this world; besides, we become attached to those whose suffering we share. If people still talk today in country cottages of Louis I of Bavaria, or Prince Rudolf, is it not because of Lola Montez and Mayerling? The drama of love is a powerful bond which often lasts over the centuries, binding together crowned kings and their humble subjects.

As I see it, nothing appears to threaten the British monarchy; its withdrawal from public affairs, the attitude of benevolent neutrality it adopts in relation to the class struggle, together with the immense popularity it enjoys on the Continent would appear to give it an excellent expectation of life. For its fate to be put in the balance, it would really have to indulge in wild excesses: tyranny, excessive spending, riotous display, freakish proclamations, participation in political movements and manoeuvres. However, short of a madman appearing in the family, I see no grounds to suppose that these disastrous circumstances should ever come to pass. Tradition, protocol, the solid fabric of a thousand unwritten laws stand as a staunch rampart against any behaviour which might hasten the ruin of the house of Windsor.

But in my opinion there remains one additional and decisive argument to convince us that the Windsors will never commit, unless unwittingly, any act which might compromise their reign: namely, the humility which springs from the sense that they have been singled out and pledged to one particular task: representing their country. England who was not created by them; she owes none of her basic structure to them, socially or economically. The Windsors are *imported* kings, and for this reason they are less likely to succumb to the intoxication of power, or the dynastic pride of a family whose ways of thought, whose life's blood make up the very texture of the land.

To all we have just said may be added one thing more. It would take a revolution to overset the house of Windsor. Now, revolution seems to have fled the shores of our old Continent, banished forever, maybe, by the refrigerator, the washing machine and the Volkswagen. Revolution is no longer to be found in Europe, but in Cuba. In Peking.

I see no reason why, if Prince Charles is a good boy, he too should not one day be shooting pheasants at Sandringham in perfect tranquillity and delighting the popular press with his feats of sporting skill.

'Happy and Glorious. . . .'

CLIVE IRVING

Clive Irving began his career as a newspaperman and was for five years Features Editor of the *Daily Express*. From there he went to the *Observer* to supervise the revision and re-styling of the paper in 1961 and in 1962 joined the *Sunday Times* shortly after the launching of their Colour Magazine. There, as Deputy Editor, he produced specials on subjects such as the Common Market and the Space Race.

In 1964 Clive Irving became Managing Editor of the *Sunday Times* with special responsibility for developing news coverage, then a year later moved to the International Publishing Corporation as Executive Editor of their magazines. In the autumn of 1966 he worked with David Frost on the concept and editorial policy of the Frost programme. Since then he has launched his own company, Clive Irving Associates, and among other activities was a founder member of the London Television Consortium and designer of *The Times Business News* and *Saturday Review*.

THE PALACE AND THE
IMAGE MACHINE

CLIVE IRVING

The manufacture of mythical personalities for public consumption has, like most of the advanced technologies, been made into an industry by the Americans. The result is the image machine – the careful preparation of a person so that however great his exposure to the limelight only the desirable elements (which in themselves may be synthetic) will show. This process reached its most developed form with President Kennedy and his family, who became deified into the symbol of Western youth and aspiration to such an astonishing extent that its ethos spread far beyond the boundaries of America. Indeed, it was potent enough to be absorbed and exploited by Harold Wilson, a character whose true connection with John Kennedy in any way eludes the most painstaking search.

The two assassinations notwithstanding, the Kennedys became by this means American royalty, a status only finally punctured when John Kennedy's widow married Aristotle Onassis. During the Kennedy Presidency the Auchinloss family was attributed with Hanoverian influence on the slender pretext that Jacqueline Kennedy's mother married into it; if America had no royal family it was prepared to invent one. With John and Robert Kennedy gone the family is still far from an expired dynasty, and 1972 will doubtless see Edward Kennedy taking over the torch.

The Kennedys were expert at news management, even if sometimes, as in the Manchester book affair, their instinct for it gets out of control. Nevertheless the fact is, at least in the case of John Kennedy, that the image machine had something of worth to build on. Without his enormous publicity machine, without Pierre Salinger and the patronage with which the Kennedys could control the press, Nixon would have been president in 1961. And how would the Cuban missile crisis have been handled then? The image machine made the difference between narrow victory and ignominious defeat for the Kennedy election

99

campaign, and despite all its hyperbolic excesses it should be thanked for that.

Of course, such expertise could be used for malevolent ends. This intense reliance on the personalization of issues which are much more complex than one human being, the spreading of the idea that it is within the capacity of any one man to right all ills, is a dangerous simplification of the truth which reduces political issues to the importance of soap powder. It is terrifying to reflect that the image machine is still at an early stage in its use, and today's standards may well be regarded as crude in ten years' time. I wonder, too, when the public capacity to believe in its fantasies will reach saturation point. We are, I fear, far from that point yet.

I also wonder whether our own Royal Family is likely to resort to this type of persuasion. It is easy to predict circumstances in which their advisers might be tempted to consider it. Consider, first of all, the question of 'style' – the 'Kennedy style' was a phenomenon in American political life in which the White House became much more than the home of the first family. A régime whose one leisure activity had centred on the golf course was succeeded by one which set out to be an intellectual power house, which sponsored recitals by Casals, restored the neglected artistic heritage of America and invoked the poetry of Robert Frost on inauguration day.

Nobody, however charitable, could say that our present Royal Family has this kind of style, if any at all. The mainstream of British cultural life does not flow down The Mall any more than it does through Downing Street. The monarchy and the Prime Minister are unashamedly – in Mr Wilson's case even aggressively – philistine. One suspects that this is one of the factors which has contributed to the present empathy of court and prime minister.

The Duke of Edinburgh has striven to make a virtue out of this philistinism. He has become the leading propagandist for mercantile endeavour, for ruthless reforms of British management, for multilingual packing-cases, for pulling out fingers and putting in technology. For him, like the Prime Minister, the very word 'technology' is the only kind of revolution which can be endorsed because it threatens neither of their positions, a word which can be usefully dropped into every pronouncement to win the support of all modern-minded people. The Duke is obviously at home in the sweating and thrusting society of polo players, yachtsmen, and all manifestations of the spartan philosophy of Gordonstoun, and everything has been done to see that Prince Charles follows the same enthusiasms.

The Queen has inherited one of the greatest art collections in the world, and had made the gesture of making a part of it accessible to those of her subjects who know it is there and enjoy seeing it. She has herself, however, made no pretence of being devoted to it and although she is occasionally to be seen at Covent Garden and the theatre, she does not pursue such things with anything like the dedication she shows for horse-racing and the Badminton trials. She probably gets a great deal more pleasure from studying *Sporting Life* than from reading the *Guardian* and although there is now an accomplished photographer of the arts in her family, the pictures she likes best are those of herself and her family out riding.

Within the last few years the centre of gravity of the fashion world has moved from Paris to London and the mini-skirt, leather boots and plastic dresses have given this country a reputation for *chic,* not to say *kink,* which only seven years ago would have seemed as remote as a Labour government. The Queen, however, has registered none of it. She has never pretended to be what she is not, and she has never shown any sign of being able to make the best of what she has. Her clothes are without any kind of flair, and their only consistency is their dullness.

She cannot be held responsible for the architectural disaster of Buckingham Palace. The only view of it which is at all tolerable is that from the Hilton Hotel, an inadvertently egalitarian elevation which shows the Palace's best side – its back – and the gardens. From the front it is about as appealing as Caterham Barracks, though noticeably larger. None of the other royal homes has anything remotely approaching the grace of Versailles. There is no elegance in any aspect of the royal tradition. Its riches are concealed from the public gaze in galleries and libraries, contributing nothing to the quality of anyone's life.

There could not, therefore, be a more suitable case for treatment by the image machine. Something would first have to be done about the Duke's handling of newspapermen. No public relations consultants, no news-managers, no advertising agency photographers could begin the task of reconstructing the character of our monarchy unless they could be sure of sympathetic and civil treatment from him. They would have to be given the same respect as super export-salesmen or computer designers.

What would the formula be for changing the face of the monarchy? Would Mary Quant be appointed wardrobe mistress? Would there be a performance of *Marat-Sade* on the royal lawns by the Royal Shakespeare Company? Would Sandringham be sold and a marina compound be built at Chichester for yachting weekends? Would the Queen give up the racing calendar for Len Deighton thrillers and would Princess Anne be allowed to open a boutique in the King's Road? Could Buck House swing like the rest of the town? Would there be riots in the rest of Europe calling for the restoration of the monarchies to provide a new dynamic to government? And would Harold Wilson publish a book called *The Wit of The Queen*?

This may all look like a grotesque fantasy, but such things are the stock in trade of the image machine. The mere suggestion of such developments is enough to make us suddenly grateful for the Royal Family being the way it is. Because they are, above all, very ordinary people – none of them gifted in a way which makes the ardour of the royal routine a great sacrifice of thwarted talents, none of them is mad or otherwise eccentric, none of them, as far as we know, indulges the rapacious appetites which enlivened the courts of their forebears, and none falls short of the demands of a role in life which would send most of us to the limits of despair were it ours.

In the last decade the Royal Family has been extraordinarily successful in consolidating the picture of its ordinariness. There was the episode of Princess Margaret and Peter Townsend, which had a flavour of old-fashioned thwarted love and self-denying gallantry about it. There was the unhappy extravagance of the royal yacht, compensated for by its patent temperament at sea. There have been various excesses of the Duke's ill-concealed contempt for reporters. There has been the assimilation of Mr Armstrong Jones without stifling his dedication to photography. There has been the somewhat questionably precipitate transfer of power from Mr Harold Macmillan to Lord Home, which dangerously ensnared the monarch in the machinations of the Conservative party. But on the whole there has been a lowering of the temperature since the ludicrous attempt to make a slogan out of 'the second Elizabethan age' as though the accession of a young queen was in itself enough to regenerate the idea of empire. The Elizabethan cult does, however, achieve occasional revivals. The renaming of the Q4, as the *Queen Elizabeth II,* is an unfortunate throw-back, and reminds one that the sea usually brings out the worst excesses of jingoism in the British.

The choice between this and the harshly anonymous Q4 is a nice portrait in miniature of the two extremes of sentiment – one regally nostalgic, and the other a product of the technological madness which has made our phone numbers so forgettable. A ship that few people think will ever pay its way, subsidized by more than twenty million pounds of tax-payers' money, and dubbed *Queen Elizabeth II* – here again the monarchy foolishly identifies itself with profligate support for fading glories.

The initial work in puncturing the old fantasies surrounding the monarchy was done by Lord Altrincham and Mr Malcolm Muggeridge, and it is a measure of how far they have succeeded that neither would now be regarded as an untouchable – as Muggeridge once was by the BBC – because of their views. They may still be less than popular among widows in Cheltenham, but the overwhelming proportion of the population now so obviously shares their realism about the monarchy that the heresy of ten years ago is the orthodoxy of today.

The Queen's children have so successfully been kept out of the limelight that few of her subjects can remember how many there are or their names. All this seems a far cry from the day of Crawfie's maudlin memoirs of 'The Little Princesses' in *Woman's Own,* and it is doubtful now whether such trivia could ever again so successfully elevate the sales of a woman's magazine. Royal faces are no longer automatic for the covers of flagging publications, though it must be admitted that in Italy, France and Germany they still seem to have great restorative powers, whatever the substance or otherwise of the headlines over them.

The efforts of the Press Council have insulated the Royal Family from many of the old transgressions of their privacy which the long-focus lens once perpetrated. The education of Prince Charles has eluded any really informed and accurate commentary, in spite of the accessibility of his activities at Gordonstoun, in Australia and at Cambridge. Either schoolboys are less easy to bribe than they used to be, or editors really have stopped shadowing the Prince and his sister. Instead, we get occasional 'photo calls' in which selected cameramen are sent, on behalf of all the newspapers, to capture the contrived informality of the Royal Family group on one or other of their birthdays.

While this reform has made life more tolerable for the Royal Family, it is when they are acknowledged as a subject worth more serious scrutiny than that given to them by the gossip columns that the limits of the reform are exposed. And the monarchy remains a serious subject as its role evolves. We have chosen to keep it long after other nations have removed theirs; and while other monarchies have although retained become devalued by democracy, ours still retains great wealth and more influence than many suspect.

There are, I believe, sound reasons why our monarchy has not been discarded as an anachronism. But to justify this belief, it will have to exhibit adaptability to the changing realities of the life which goes on around it. It cannot find any security by allowing itself to be by-passed by the rest of the country, but nor can it ever return to past power. And one of the essential elements in this adjustment has got to be a greater tolerance towards legitimate inquiry than it has shown, a greater expectancy of such inquiry, and a greater appreciation of the positive value of the right kind of publicity. Concealment of private lives is all very well – but there is a great deal of information about the monarchy which ought to be public knowledge yet which is still jealously guarded by people misguided enough to believe that obstruction is in the best interest of the family they serve.

It is a euphemism frequently employed by newspapers to blame the court's 'advisers' for misjudgements at the Palace, when quite often the fault is probably the Queen's or Prince Philip's. Nevertheless it is an important function of the 'advisers' to decide when to talk to the press and how much talking should be done. Their attitude is constantly defensive. Rare have been the initiatives from the Palace itself which have led to a better understanding of its problems and its role. The Press Council's work has been usually to respond after mistakes have been made, rather than to be allowed to advise on how they might never happen.

The monarchy as an institution is as open to questioning as

any other, and one aspect of it which will be under continued scrutiny is its finances, how they are spent and where they come from. There may not be the same need now to question how the money is spent as there was when Sir Charles Dilke made allegations of waste and nepotism in 1871, much to the detriment of his career, but lack of information adds to suspicion and the Civil List is less than useless in any attempt to put royal expenditure to a 'cost-effectiveness' test. This is surely a legitimate examination to make, for it is one which the whole country is having to make of itself, and the monarchy cannot be immune from it. The Duke of Edinburgh is very free with his advice to British industry on how it can improve its efficiency; let him apply the same standards to his own household, where the simple provision of a pot of tea requires a level of manning in excess of that of even the newspaper industry.

Of course, the royal palaces were not designed for an age of time-and-motion study, but other similarly inefficient structures have been redesigned to improve economy and comfort at the same time. There might well be a reduction in their number without inflicting either hardship or a level of sacrifice which would undermine the still essential pretensions which the monarchy must retain if it is to have any meaning.

The best basis for criticism of this kind would be facts to enable an accurate measure to be taken of the legitimacy of royal expenditure. However, these facts cannot at the moment be prised from the Buckingham Palace Press Office, nor can any details of the various efforts made over the past few years to improve the machinery which serves the Queen. The Press Office itself is a vital part of that machinery and *it* has not been giving value for money. The solid wall which this department has erected against the search for anything above the kind of vacuous 'advice' which it dispenses on the superficialities of the life of the Royal Family will have to be broken down if further misrepresentations are to be avoided. At the moment there is little sign of it.

Somebody in the Palace has to learn to distinguish between the kind of irresponsible rubbish which Continental newspapers peddle and the genuine search for more information about the problems of the monarchy. This does not presuppose that such inquiries are a threat to the monarchy, or that they will end in arguments seeking to render its role neuter. There is no harm, and there may even be some benefit, in the Duke acting as a salesman for Britain, but whatever he says about efficiency will be discredited so long as it can be proved to be hypocrisy.

The best case for the monarchy is apparent simply by considering the alternative. Its value becomes persuasive for me in the way that it acts as a buffer between the armed forces and the political machine. We have, fortunately, no tradition in Britain of generals seeking to become the head of state – an Eisenhower or a de Gaulle is, thankfully, an impossible phenomenon for us. This works because of a curious and inimitably British paradox – although the allegiance of the armed forces is to a person, the monarch, this figurehead is really an abstraction and therefore the focus for patriotism is not political in its nature. It is, however, all the more meaningful for that. However much the generals may be disenchanted by their political masters, they cannot enforce their views with a *coup d'etat* because it is not the Prime Minister but the crown which they would have to topple, and such an event is unthinkable.

Even when a political decision introduces a great division in the country over the true shape of patriotism, as with the Rhodesian crisis, the Queen has managed to remain neutral and it is impossible to gauge where her sympathies might lie. However extreme the feelings of the *ultras* supporting the Smith régime, they still swear their fidelity to the throne, while at the same time Mr Wilson is able to classify the Rhodesians as rebels against the authority of the sovereign without any contradiction being apparent to either side. No republican President would have survived the strains of such ambiguity.

Because of this, it is probably just as well if whatever reforms in the relationship between the Palace and the press do occur, they do not include a statement on the weekly meeting between the Queen and the Prime Minister. It has been suggested that an unexpected degree of *rapport* has flowered between the two since Mr Wilson came to power. But I remember hearing similar stories about Sir Alec ('she admires his patrician calm') and Harold Macmillan ('she regards him as a great statesman'). In the case of Mr Wilson it has been alleged that his lucidity and directness, not to mention the inevitable pragmatism, are the qualities which have disarmed the presumed prejudice towards socialism. It would indeed be unusual if the impression was allowed to get around that there was no real communication between a prime minister and the monarch and in this respect at least one cannot fault the record of the Palace Press Office.

Perhaps the largest public relations problem looming for the Palace is the future life of the Prince of Wales. The memories invoked by this particular title are not fortunate, and there is at least one parallel already obvious between Charles and Edward VII – he, too, will probably get through a large part of his adult life before succeeding to the throne. Gordonstoun has been usefully remote; Cambridge is much less so. One hopes that he will not be provided with a portable ghetto for his time as a student, and that he will be allowed both by the Palace and by the press to live something approximating to a normal life, so that the experience can give the benefits intended. I say approximating to, because it would be too idealistic to suppose that his life can be typical in every respect.

So far the Cambridge experiment has worked. The press has not been silly about it. The Prince has enjoyed himself, at work and with amateur dramatics. He has had to do without the libertarian delights of many of his contemporaries, but the routine has not been too severe. He gave an interview to BBC radio which showed something of the penalty of his burden – already his views had a circumspect middle-aged ring; one suspects his father as the source of his skill with political bromides. These are the years in which his image is hardening up, ready for the tricky public role in Wales.

More important than this phase, though, will be his ultimate role. No particular aptitude is apparent from his studies so far – he is probably a healthily average performer and though his training so far has been in the mould of his father it would seem that he is less devoted to extrovert activity than Prince Philip, showing more the reflective qualities of his mother. It is useless to speculate about how best he can make a contribution not only to the monarchy (and he will obviously relieve his mother of some of her routine duties) but to the life of Britain and the Commonwealth. He may share his father's taste for globe-trotting, in which case the Commonwealth could be his special field. But wherever he goes and whatever he does he will be deeper into the royal goldfish bowl than anything he has experienced so far.

If this problem is not handled properly, it could well lead to a new crisis between the press and the Palace, and if the Press Office remains organized as it now is there certainly will be trouble. It is not only the competence of the Press Office which is at issue, but its strength and place within the total administrative and advisory machine which serves the Queen.

The traditional attitude to the place of the Press Office has been inadequate to the problem for a long while. As with much of the other advice which the Queen receives, that on press relations has always come from dedicated amateurs rather than from people with a more relevant training than honourable military service provides. The secretaries and equerries concerned may well have an instinctive feeling for the repression of information, and they certainly have practised this in a courtly and civilized manner. But this will not be any good.

The case for the monarchy, to establish its continuing relevance in a rapidly changing society, will have to be prepared and advanced by professionals, combining a sympathy for their subject with a cynical realism about all the opportunities for misrepresentation and exploitation which the monarchy can fall victim to. It is a task much more complex than simply answering telephone calls with a bland indifference to legitimate requests for facts. It requires a fine sense of anticipation, of being able to judge the consequences – often second or third stage consequences – of royal activities. It should be informed by a knowledge of the technical problems, many and varied, of all the communications media. And its ethic should be one of fearless honesty.

If it acquires this degree of professionalism, as it must, the Palace must at the same time prevent the greater excesses of the image machine. There is a rich store of material to sate such an operation, and therefore the temptation would be strong. But the construction around our Royal Family of a modern public relations fantasy, so easy to do, would in the end be an act of self-destruction. The monarchy needs to emulate nothing, because it works. But it must be seen to work, and submit itself to being seen in ways more fundamental to its meaning than royal tours.

We should have the same right to scrutinize the machinery of the monarchy that we exercise over government machinery. The Palace must be prepared to open up its books, to allow us to see not only how much value for money we get out of the monarchy but also to make sure it applies to itself the same standards which it urges on all the other representatives of this country. At the moment the Queen and her husband choose the ground on which they appear in public, very much according to tradition and also according to the neolithic advice of the press department. As a result, the grind of public appearances is as tiring as ever, a burden which becomes greater as they grow older. A certain amount of personal, face to face contacts is obviously valuable. But the accepted round, relentlessly followed, designed to touch every burgher in his lifetime, is not only beyond the energy of anybody, but also ignores that today there are very effective ways of getting across to millions of people without actually shaking their hands. If only the Queen could really appear as she is, in an unrehearsed, informal and involved situation discussing, for example, her ideas of the national purpose with others who have a chance of shaping it – all this in front of television cameras – how much more value it would have than the appallingly contrived and useless Christmas broadcast. The Duke, and now the Prince of Wales, could also be used very effectively in a similar way, and if they really want to justify their existence they ought to try it. The chances are that it would work, and if by doing it they finally removed the psychological moat dividing the monarchy from the people, so much the better.

PAUL JOHNSON

Paul Johnson was born in 1928 and was educated at Stonyhurst and Magdalen College, Oxford. He worked for three and a half years in Paris as Assistant Editor of *Réalités*, a French monthly magazine, and as Paris Correspondent for the *New Statesman*. In 1955 he joined the staff of the *New Statesman* and he has been Editor since 1965. He is married with four children.

PUBLICATIONS
The Suez War, Journey into Chaos (political study of the Middle East), *Left of Centre, Merrie England* (novels).

THE POLITICAL POWER OF THE MONARCHY

PAUL JOHNSON

The question: How much power should the sovereign possess? cannot be answered until we examine a further question: How much power does the sovereign possess? There is a good deal of confusion on this point, even among politicians of some seniority and experience. Statements such as 'The sovereign reigns but does not rule' are widely accepted but rarely subjected to critical examination in the light of the documentary evidence. Bagehot's famous statement, that the powers of the monarch are limited to the right to be consulted, the right to encourage and the right to warn, is seriously misleading. It was certainly untrue in his own day, as the publication of Queen Victoria's letters conclusively showed. But later monarchs, particularly George V, were encouraged to read and accept Bagehot, and his statement is now much closer to actual practice than when he wrote it. Even so, it needs to be heavily qualified.

Since the establishment of the Hanoverian dynasty, the doctrine of ministerial responsibility has become the dominant fact of our constitution; the king can do no wrong, and therefore ministers must be held responsible for all acts of the crown; as they are held responsible for such acts, they must decide them. In practice, however, their rights in this respect have been limited by the personal determination of the sovereign. George I and George II took little interest in English politics and were chiefly concerned with Hanoverian affairs. All the same, their ministers, especially Walpole, derived their authority mainly through their influence at court. George III, who was able, energetic and passionately concerned with the details of domestic politics, had no difficulty in vastly increasing the power of the monarchy; the decline of his authority in the later part of his reign was due more to ill-health than any other factor. Not only did he make and unmake governments and veto the legislative proposals of his ministers, he performed executive acts without advice, chiefly in the sphere of appointments in the church, the army, the household and the peerage. For example, in several letters to Lord North he instructed his prime minister to make certain ecclesiastic appointments and transfers; he appointed one Archbishop of Canterbury during a ministerial interregnum and another against the express advice of his Prime Minister, Pitt. Again, one of his Secretaries-at-War, Lord Barrington, in a letter to the King, wrote that he did not trouble to come to London on news of an important army vacancy, 'recollecting that when you are pleased to give anything immediately away, Your Majesty commonly sends your directions in writing'. In the Irish army, the King determined all promotions above the rank of colonel, and occasionally junior appointments too. Peerages and knighthoods were given or witheld at the King's discretion.

The decline of the personal monarchical power exercised by George III was due to a number of factors, ably summarized in the last of Professor Richard Pares' Ford Lectures.[1] Neither George IV nor, still less, William IV, carried anything like the weight of their father in political circles; both were indolent and disliked detail; both were held in low esteem by the public. Ministers were able to enforce their will against royal inclinations much more frequently. George IV postponed, but could not ultimately prevent, Catholic Emancipation; William IV's conditional promise to create peers to secure the passage of the Reform Bill marked a royal capitulation to the supremacy of the House of Commons. The rapid decline of patronage gradually destroyed the direct parliamentary power of the crown. From 1742-1830, the government – that is ministers selected and maintained by the King – did not lose a single general election. The resignation of the Tories in 1830, with the passage of the Reform Bill two years later, formed a watershed. Henceforward the monarch had to deal, not with individual aristocrats, heading loosely organized and shifting factions, but with the acknowledged leaders of great parties, increasingly capable of fighting and winning parliamentary elections on a national scale.

This process did not occur overnight, but the growth of the modern party system inevitably obliged the monarch to select ministers from those who demonstrably carried the weight of public opinion behind them. The Reform Bill added 217,000 to

[1] *King George III and the Politicians*, by Richard Pares, 1953.

an existing electorate of 500,000; within the next generation a further 600,000 qualified to vote. 1834 saw the first General Election manifesto; 1841 the first occasion in which a General Election returned to power an opposition with a massive and dependable majority. The number of contested individual elections, fought on party lines, steadily increased: in 1859, 101; in 1865, 204; in 1868, 277; in 1880, 352. Finally in 1877 the creation of the National Liberal Federation inaugurated modern machine politics and with them modern concepts of party discipline. The power of the monarch was destroyed by the party system; and so long as this system remains strong, especially if organized on a two-party basis, the direct political power of the monarch will remain minimal.

All the same, within this general proposition, sovereigns have continued to exercise some power and much influence. Queen Victoria's correspondence shows that, on a very large number of occasions, she sought, sometimes successfully, to influence acts of the executive, and that she frequently got her way over appointments. So long as the Prince Consort was alive, her interference was largely confined to foreign affairs and was conducted in accordance with what her husband imagined to be systematic constitutional doctrine; after his death, and especially after 1868, she became increasingly a party monarch, throwing her weight repeatedly and forcefully against the Liberals and in favour of the Conservatives. In 1880 and again in 1886 she tried to prevent the formation of a Gladstone government, on the second occasion by means of an intrigue with Conservative and dissident Liberal politicians, and in a manner which all authorities have since judged to be rankly unconstitutional.[1] Only Gladstone's long-suffering esteem for the institution of monarchy prevented an open constitutional crisis from developing.

The Queen's political ventures might have been more successful if they had been motivated less by blatant personal prejudices and more by consistent political opinions; as it was, most of them came to nothing. But, like her grandfather, she was able to influence a large number of official and ecclesiastical appointments, and in some cases the selection of ministers. Her view of her prerogative is perhaps best expressed in a letter she wrote

[1] See Sir Ivor Jenning's *Cabinet Government*, second edition (1951), pp. 32-35.

to her Private Secretary, Sir Henry Ponsonby, in 1880, after it had become clear that the Liberals had won an overwhelming electoral victory:

'What the Queen is especially anxious to have impressed on Lords Hartington and Granville is, firstly, that Mr Gladstone *she* can have nothing to do with, for she considers his whole conduct since '76 to have been one series of violent, passionate invective against and abuse of Lord Beaconsfield, and that *he* caused the Russian war, and made the task of the Government of this country most difficult in times of the greatest difficulty and anxiety, and did all to try and prevent England from holding the position which, thanks to Lord Beaconsfield's firmness, has been restored to her . . . she wishes, however, to support the new Government and to show them confidence, as she has hitherto done all her Governments, but that *this must entirely depend* on their conduct. There must be no democratic leaning, no attempt to change the Foreign policy (and the Continent are terribly alarmed), no change in India, no hasty retreat from Afghanistan, and *no* cutting down of estimates . . . Mr Lowe she could *not* accept as a minister. Sir C. Dilke she would only and unwillingly consent to having a *subordinate office* if absolutely necessary.'[1]

On none of the salient points did the Queen, in fact, get her way. But I think it can fairly be argued that her attitudes acted as a continual brake on Liberal reformist legislation and helped to determine the political balance of Gladstone's cabinets, which never accurately reflected the radical leanings of his parliamentary majorities.

To a greater or lesser extent, all Victoria's prime ministers – with the exception of Sir Robert Peel, the most determined and masterful of them all – found it politic to yield to some of the Queen's demands. One of the reasons why she preferred Disraeli to Gladstone was that the former regularly provided her with details of secret cabinet debates, including the views of individual ministers – a practice which Gladstone rightly regarded as unconstitutional and declined to follow. One further point is worth noting. Some of the Queen's premiers were uncomfortably aware, especially after Albert's death, that the Queen feared she might become insane, like her grandfather. An insane monarch poses

[1] *Letters of Queen Victoria*, second series Vol. III.

fearful problems for any government, and they were therefore more inclined to yield to her rabid entreaties rather than risk provoking a mental crisis.

Edward VII behaved in a much more circumspect fashion than his mother and set the modern constitutional pattern. Though by nature conservative, he was very much a man of the world, with a range of personal friends throughout the political spectrum. He remained on friendly terms with Sir Charles Dilke, despite the latter's republican opinions and, even more surprisingly, despite his public disgrace; he was a firm friend of Sir Henry Campbell-Bannerman, the leader of the Liberals, although Sir Henry's views on the Boer War were thoroughly repulsive to the court establishment. Edward raised no difficulties when the Liberals returned to power in 1905, and his only known interference in ministerial appointments was to point out to Mr Asquith, the Prime Minister, that his Lord President of the Council, Lord Tweedmouth, was clearly insane. The vast majority of ministerial communications to him, even in the field of foreign affairs, where his knowledge was considerable, he merely initialled *approved*. As a monarchical diplomatist, he enjoyed very considerable success; but in this work, both at home and during his European tours, he invariably acted in accordance with ministerial advice.

Edward's heir, George V, had to face several constitutional crises of great complexity, in one of which his own acts were decisive. Over the Parliament Act crisis of 1911, he scrupulously followed the ministerial advice given by Mr Asquith, and his behaviour cannot be faulted; he played a personal role in the Irish crisis in 1914, but likewise on his Prime Minister's advice; again, in the 1916 cabinet crisis, which led to the formation of the Lloyd George government, he behaved with complete propriety, though his personal wish was clearly that Asquith should remain premier. But he certainly sought to interfere in military appointments during the First World War. He played a major role in the dismissal of French and his replacement by Haig, and later sought to protect Haig, Robertson and Jellicoe from dismissal – successfully in the first case.

The King's major exercise of political power, however, occurred during the 1931 crisis. At the time he was fiercely attacked for unconstitutional behaviour by Professor Laski, and fiercely defended by one of the chief actors, Sir Herbert Samuel. The crux is this. When Macdonald resigned, should the King simply have sent for Mr Baldwin, as the leader of the opposition; or was he justified in persuading Macdonald to remain as leader of a national government? The King clearly received advice to follow this latter course, from both Baldwin and, more clearly, from Samuel, the leader of the Liberals. But the direct and fore-seeable effect of the King's act was to break up the Labour party and to secure a predominantly Conservative House of Commons for an entire decade. Moreover, it is clear from the minute made by his Private Secretary, Sir Clive Wigram, that the King already favoured this course of action before he received advice from the two other party leaders, for immediately after Macdonald tendered his resignation,

'The King impressed on the Prime Minister that he was the only man to lead the country through this crisis and hoped he would reconsider the situation. His Majesty told him that the Conservatives and Liberals would support him in restoring the confidence of foreigners in the financial stability of the country.'

Naturally, all three party leaders quickly fell in with the King's wishes. At no point did he seek to discover the views or advice of the majority of Macdonald's cabinet. If it is argued that the King's behaviour was constitutionally correct, then it must also be conceded that the constitution still permits a decisive political role to the monarch in moments of crisis.

Moreover, it is axiomatic that this role will be exercised in favour of the conservative forces in the country. King George was thirty-five when Queen Victoria died, and remained, in all essentials, a Victorian gentleman. All his training, instincts and inclinations militated in favour of stability and against innovation. He was surrounded by men of similar views. In Mr John Gore's personal memoir,[1] a list of his friends is given: the Dukes of Devonshire, Portland and Roxburghe, Lords Revelstoke, Derby, Rosebery, Crewe, Durham, Lonsdale, Sefton, Annaly, Chesham, Lovat, Somerleyton, Downe; Lord Herbert Vane-Tempest and the Mackintosh of Mackintosh; Archbishops Lang and Davidson; Deans Blackburne and Baillie; Canons Green and Sheppard, and Prebendary Percival; Haig, Jellicoe, Kitchener, Byng, Beatty,

---

[1] *King George V, a personal memoir*, by John Gore, John Murray (1941).

Plumer, Robertson, Smith-Dorrien, the Brigadier who managed his racing stable, and the three admirals who commanded his yacht; Sir Edward Peacock, a partner in Barings; Sir Bernard Halsey-Bircham, his lawyer; Lord Hankey, Sir Robert Vansittart, the Maharajah of Jodhpur, Sir Pertab Singh and the Maharajah of Bikanir; together with a number of senior servants from his estates. With one or two exceptions all were Tories or inclined in that direction. Among lady friends, of whom he had few, the memorialist lists Mme d'Hautpoul, Lady Algernon Gordon-Lennox, Lady Mar, Lady Meux and Mrs Fetherstonehaugh, 'who were certainly able', Mr Gore adds in all seriousness, 'to help him to assimilate a little of the spirit of the post-war age and to appreciate the claims of youth'.

If Edward VII established the constitutional pattern of the modern British monarchy, George V set its tone: correct, establishmentarian, conservative in all things, a brake – limited in force but persistent in application – to political experiment and social change. It is significant that one of the principal charges against his successor, Edward VIII, was that he drew his friends, both male and female, from an altogether different circle from his father's: what might be termed the international smart set, as opposed to the traditional landowning aristocracy. Mr Baldwin expressed his anxieties on this score even before the new king succeeded; and Archibishop Cosmo Gordon Lang records in his diary a talk with Edward immediately after his accession, in which he was distressed to learn that the King knew only two clergymen, and those not very well![1] There can have been no real fear that Edward would align himself with the radical forces – the incident in South Wales, in which he expressed sympathy with the unemployed miners without reference to his ministers, was of no great importance – but there was an uneasy feeling that the new monarch was 'undependable' and open to 'dangerous' influences. Both Baldwin and Lang much preferred his brother, whom they recognized as being cast in a mould similar to George V; and it was a relief to them when Edward insisted on marrying Mrs Simpson, and thus made his abdication inevitable. For it is a paradox that parliament had insisted on a strict control of the monarch's choice in marriage long before it had established

[1] *Cosmo Gordon Lang*, by J. G. Lockhart, p. 395.

effective curbs on his political powers: Edward thus challenged his ministers on ground where he was weakest, and his defeat, from the outset, was certain.

George VI followed the pattern of his father in all essentials, though he was a less opinionated and forceful man. He played a significant political role only on two occasions: in 1940 and in 1951. When Neville Chamberlain resigned, his personal wish and his political instinct was to send for Lord Halifax – thus reflecting prevailing establishment opinion – and he commissioned Winston Churchill to form a government with some reluctance. In the autumn of 1951 a degree of pressure on his part persuaded Mr Attlee to hold a general election which resulted in a Conservative victory and a long spell of Tory rule. Attlee it is true had only a tiny majority; but it was a working one, and every political and economic consideration should have told him to postpone an appeal to the country. According to his own account, his decision was influenced by his desire to meet the King's convenience; but this may be interpreted as an *apologia* for what was an undoubted error of judgement on his part. All the incident really shows is that the monarch may play a residual role in the prime minister's most valuable single prerogative – the right to determine the timing of the election.

So far as we can judge, Queen Elizabeth II has conformed strictly to the constitutional practices laid down by Edward VII, and to the social attitudes of her father and grandfather. She made a 'suitable' marriage, and has encouraged other members of her family to do likewise; she is strictly conformist in religion and interests herself in the doings of the clergy; she performs her role as head of the Commonwealth with great assiduity; she reads her official papers carefully and is polite to her ministers, whatever their political colour; she goes through the democratic motions and entertains a wide variety of her subjects at informal lunch parties; but she selects her private friends from exactly the same circle as George V; she shoots birds in Norfolk and stalks deer in Scotland; she ardently upholds the traditional royal patronage of the turf and bloodstock; and in her public utterances she confines herself to the plain diet of clichés and platitudes prepared by the royal secretariat.

How much power does she exert? She is strict in the observance of constitutional forms, and insists on her right to be consulted, to encourage and to warn. She has been 'in office' now for over seventeen years, much longer than any of her ministers, and thus has a continuity of knowledge about public affairs which occasionally gives her a useful advantage in her dealings with the government – an advantage which will grow the longer she lives. In certain spheres – clerical appointments, honours, public ceremonies, uniforms, military organization and the like – she has clear views which must always be taken into account. If, as has happened on at least two occasions, an emergency meeting of the Privy Council is held while she is out of London, she insists that ministers must go to her, instead of vice versa, whatever the administrative inconvenience. All the same, the power of the sovereign has continued to decline during her reign, especially in one vital aspect.

By far the most important power enjoyed by the modern British monarchy, until recently, had been the right to select a prime minister. The only limitation on the monarch's unrestricted choice was that the person selected should be able to command a majority of the House of Commons, and so carry on the business of government. As a rule, following a general election, the choice was automatic (though Victoria did not take this view in 1880). Again, when there is already a clearly designated successor to replace a retiring prime minister, the monarch was not called upon to exercise a choice. Asquith, Balfour, Chamberlain and Eden were all appointed as a matter of course. Equally, when a party has a precise and constitutional procedure for electing its leader, the monarch must accept the man so chosen, for there would be a presumption that anyone else would not receive the requisite support. But when the absence of such a procedure created an element of doubt, the onus of choice fell squarely on the monarch's shoulders.

What is more, though the monarch was clearly prudent to take advice before choosing, there was no obligation to do so, still less to seek it from any particular quarter. There is no foundation for the myth that the monarch must consult the retiring prime minister. Queen Victoria did not do so in 1894 and seems to have appointed Rosebery without taking advice of any kind; Edward VII did not consult Campbell-Bannerman in 1908, and in 1916 George V sent for Lloyd George at the suggestion of Bonar Law, then Colonial Secretary, in his capacity as

Leader of the Conservatives. In 1923, Bonar Law, after careful inquiries, concluded that it was not his duty to offer advice. In 1940 we know exactly what happened, as it is recorded in the King's diary. First, the King suggested Halifax. Chamberlain objected, not on the grounds that he was unsuitable but because he was unwilling. The diary continues:

'Then I knew that there was only one person I could send for to form a government who had the confidence of the country, and that was Winston. I asked Chamberlain his advice, and he told me Winston was the man to send for.'

The whole passage makes it clear that the King, while courteous and deferential to Chamberlain, was carefully preserving his prerogative.

In the case of Mr Macmillan's appointment in 1957, we do not know whether Eden was consulted (the presumption is that he was not; but it is possible that, in view of his health, he declined to advise). The Queen's choice, however, seems to have been made as the result of advice given by Lord Salisbury and Sir Winston Churchill and soundings carried out by the Lord Chancellor and the Tory whips. All these precedents make it clear that the role of the prime minister in choosing his successor has been limited or non-existent, and that in any event his advice had never been mandatory.

The events of October 1963, therefore, mark a constitutional watershed. When the state of Mr Macmillan's health made his resignation inevitable, there were three contenders for the succession – Mr Butler, Mr Maudling and Lord Hailsham. Mr Butler seemingly commanded the greatest measure of support, especially in the Cabinet; there were strong objections to him in some quarters, but these were unlikely to prevent him forming a government once he had been commissioned by the Queen to do so. In particular, his ability to form a government was certain once Hailsham and Maudling had agreed to serve under him.

In the light of this, and of all the precedents, Mr Macmillan's behaviour appears truly extraordinary. He was an elderly man who had just undergone a serious operation and had recently been under heavy sedation. A more diffident statesman might well have concluded that, in all the circumstances, he might honourably have discharged himself from tendering advice in so complex a matter and, still more, of assembling and collating the evidence on which that advice would be based. This was the view Bonar Law took in 1923. But Mr Macmillan suffered from no such doubts or inhibitions. From the very start he seems to have determined that his advice should not only be given, but given in all its plenitude. The document he eventually presented (and indeed read) to the Queen has been described as 'magisterial'.

It appears that Macmillan presented to the Cabinet a paper describing in detail the lines on which party soundings should be conducted. But there is some doubt whether the Cabinet formally approved the paper; in any case, if the procedure itself was to be invested with the weight of Cabinet authority, the Cabinet clearly had an equal right to be shown, and to check, its findings before they were presented to the Queen. The Cabinet, it seems, was given no such opportunity. No one outside Mr Macmillan's personal secretariat saw the memorandum in its final form.

What is more, it appeared at the last moment that the memorandum – which recommended Lord Home to succeed – did not reflect majority opinion within the cabinet. As noted above, if any two of the three principal contenders formally agreed to serve under the third, a compromise candidate, such as Lord Home, became unnecessary, and the crisis was resolved. It could then be argued that the Home candidacy had served its turn by forcing the three principals to agree among themselves. This, indeed, happened on the evening of Thursday, October 17, when Hailsham and Maudling declared that they were opposed to Lord Home and pledged themselves to serve under Mr Butler. Mr Redmayne, the Chief Whip, was asked to convey the information to Mr Macmillan. When it was learnt, by the early hours of Friday, October 18, that Mr Macmillan still intended to recommend Lord Home, the news of the Tripartite Agreement was telephoned, at 7 a.m., to Sir Michael Adeane, the Queen's Private Secretary.

It is at this point that the Queen allowed her most important remaining prerogative to lapse. She was under no obligation to follow Mr Macmillan's advice, however presented, or indeed to ask for it at all. By the morning of October 18 she knew that there was some dubiety about the advice. Had Mr Macmillan been tendering formal and constitutional advice, she would of course have had no alternative but to accept it. But the procedure adopted makes it quite clear that the advice was informal. Mr

Macmillan's letter of resignation was taken to the Palace on the morning of October 18 by his secretary, Mr Bligh; the Queen came to the hospital and accepted it in person; she *then* asked for advice – from a man who was now a private individual and no longer in a constitutional position to accept responsibility for her acts. If there was any question of the validity of Mr Macmillan's advice, it was surely the Queen's duty to take a second opinion. Instead, she acted with unusual speed, and Lord Home had already been summoned to the Palace, and had agreed to try to form a government, by lunch-time.

No doubt the Queen, by personal inclination, preferred the choice of Lord Home. But, from the point of view of the monarchy her behaviour was imprudent, to say the least. She had created a precedent in which the retiring Prime Minister was allowed to dictate the choice of his successor. She thus allowed her prerogative, so jealously preserved by her predecessor, to lapse. What is more, this lapse was formalized in 1965, when the Conservative Party adopted a method of electing their leader, in or out of office. A great section of the Tories never became reconciled to Lord Home as leader; the way in which he was chosen, publicly denounced by Mr Macleod as a conspiracy by the 'magic circle', was widely, and eventually universally, recognized by the Tories as unsatisfactory. Hence, as a direct result of the Queen's action, the monarch no longer has a say in the selection of the prime minister, *provided the two-party system continues to operate.*

This is a very important proviso. As we have seen, it was the rise of the two-party system, strengthened by the adoption of universal suffrage and by the growth of highly organized party machines which, more than any other factor, ended the direct political powers of the monarch. The last vestige of them vanished in 1965, when the Tories followed Labour in adopting an elective leadership. So long as the two-party system maintains itself, the monarch is constitutionally a cypher, though he or she can exert a certain influence on ministerial decisions. But if the two-party system breaks down, if a multiplicity of parties arises, with the consequent need for fluctuating coalition governments, the political powers of the monarch will, indeed must, revive. It is up to the politicians to provide clear choices, and for the public to make them; otherwise, the monarch, the residual arbiter, must step into the vacuum.

ON HER MAJESTY'S DIPLOMATIC SERVICE

GEOFFREY KIRK

This essay originated in a BBC television interview when I was British Ambassador to the Central American Republic of El Salvador. I was told by the interviewer that I was the 'personal representative of the British Government'; to which I replied that I was the personal representative of the Queen. My reply was strictly correct, as an ambassador is by tradition the personal representative of one sovereign to another. From a practical point of view in the present age this may seem to be a fine distinction, as a British Ambassador must act on the instructions of his government; but the nomenclature remains and the usual title is 'Her Britannic Majesty's Ambassador' rather than 'British Ambassador'. This title is impressive and sounds well; but the habit of some British Government departments of addressing envelopes to 'H.B.M. Ambassador, San Salvador' *tout court* can cause difficulties and it is to the credit of the Salvadorean Post Office that such letters have generally been delivered.

It is obvious that for the greater part of his time a British Ambassador acts on behalf of his government and carries out its orders. In his representational functions however he represents the Queen. On his appointment he is received in audience by the Queen and goes through the ceremony of kissing hands. Soon after his arrival in the country to which he is posted he presents a personal letter of recommendation from the Queen to the head of state. This is known as his credentials and until they have been presented he is not recognized as an ambassador. While his reception by the Queen is private and informal, he presents his credentials with the full ceremony of bands and salutes. In my case, in order to do justice to the occasion, I wore my heavy blue uniform, with sword and feathered hat – an uncomfortable get-up at noon in the tropics. I was met at my house by the Chief of Protocol and escorted, with the senior members of my staff, to the Presidential House. After a progression of bows, I was greeted by the President and handed him my credentials. I then presented my staff and sat on the sofa for a short and formal talk.

After further bows I retreated downstairs and stood to attention while a military band played the Salvadorean national anthem and 'God Save the Queen'. The ceremony over, I returned to my house and stood the Chief of Protocol and my staff a well-earned glass of champagne. I was now a recognized ambassador.

The representational functions of an ambassador are many and sometimes exhausting. He must represent the Queen at a wide range of ceremonies; such as the handing over of the Presidency (an affair which lasts five hours or more), formal sessions of the Legislative Assembly, the bestowal of decorations on other people, official receptions, the laying of wreaths and many other occasions; not to mention the receptions given on their national days by every other country represented in the capital. All this is part of the pattern of diplomatic life and to neglect it would be discourteous; it is the oil which eases the working of diplomatic business and is not so much a waste of time as it appears to be.

Having spent most of the past twenty years abroad, it is understandable that I should look at the monarchy from a distance and invest it as symbol with more significance than do many of my fellow countrymen who live at home. Seen from a distance, the turbulence and disruption of politics is less easy to understand and more disturbing than when experienced close at hand. Also, because it was my job, I probably appreciated and understood Salvadorean politics better than I did British. An expatriate is apt to attach greater value to whatever represents the whole of his country as distinct from its conflicting parts. Roughly one half of the people in Britain are generally opposed to any government that is in power: and the minister from whom an ambassador takes his instructions is not necessarily sympathetic. It is frequently more satisfying to feel that one represents the Queen.

My own experience is that British expatriates in general feel the same way as I do and often more strongly. People who have made their homes in a foreign country while retaining their British nationality see the monarchy as an ideal Britain which they have left behind, frequently in a changing world which they neither like nor understand. One friend of mine, now in his middle seventies, came to Central America in the early 1920s after serving in the First World War. Although he has made his home in El Salvador and amassed a considerable fortune, he remains the most patriotic old boy imaginable, an ardent monarchist who can scarcely conceive of the England of the 1960s. Although he visits England every year or so, his deepest memories are those of the hardships and friendships of 1914-18: old-fashioned perhaps, but not to be despised. There are many like him and the local British communities, including the embassies, depend a great deal on their kindness and generosity. For these people and for many other expatriate Britons the most important public event of the year is the Queen's birthday, which is celebrated by a large reception in most British embassies. In El Salvador, we were given a dispensation to hold the party in the dry season, in March or April, so as to make full use of the large embassy garden. There are generally about five or six hundred people present: all the members of the British community who can come, and the remainder Salvadoreans and members of the Diplomatic Corps. Towards the end, after a call for silence, the orchestra plays 'God Save the Queen' and the Salvadorean national anthem; and the Ambassador proposes the toast of the Queen. I have done this for seven years and have always been moved by the reaction of the guests, both British and foreign. Anyone who doubts the emotional appeal of the monarchy should attend one of these parties.

Although the arguments for and against the monarchy are outside the scope of this particular essay, it is difficult to write on such a subject without at least trying to justify one's ideas. It seems to me that, of the various forms of state organization, the British monarchy as it at present exists is the one which should cause the least dispute. It has developed through the centuries, with but one short interruption, and has adapted itself successfully to the changing political needs of the country. An elected president would either be a nonentity or else would combine the attributes of head of state with that of head of government: both would divide rather than unite the country, and the second even more than the first. A republic may be a logical form of state organization; but it would be a wanton act to destroy an institution which is woven into the history of the country without being very sure that the alternative would make for greater unity and cohesion. In the present disintegrating age, these are virtues which are easier to destroy than to recreate. The Queen, as the continuing symbol of the country, has an emotional significance which no temporary president can hope to have; and seven years' service in a republic has not encouraged me to hold a different opinion.

HENRY LUCE III

Henry Luce III was born in New York City in 1925. He attended Brooks School in North Andover, Mass., graduating in 1942, and Yale University, graduating in 1948 with a BA degree. He was on active naval duty from May 1943 to June 1946, during which time he saw service aboard a a destroyer escort in the Pacific theatre, with the rank of Lieutenant j.g.

After the war he served on the staff of the Commission on Organization of the Executive Branch of the Government from February 1948 to March 1949 and then worked as a reporter for the Cleveland Press, covering the police and federal beats. He joined the staff of Time Inc. in April 1951, served successively as *Time* correspondent in Washington and *Time* contributing editor in New York. In 1956 he became head of the company's New Building Department which was engaged in planning and supervising construction of the Time & Life Building on Rockefeller Centre. After holding various posts within the company organization he joined *Time-Life News Service* as its London Bureau Chief in March 1966. Currently, he is publisher of *Fortune* magazine and is also Vice-President and Member of the Board of Directors, Time Inc.

MONARCHY: THE VITAL STRAND

HENRY LUCE III

'What is the function of the monarchy?' A fair enough question it would seem. At least it is to my American way of thinking. Function is directed toward a purpose, and the American task-oriented attitude tends to hold that all human institutions and activities have a purpose. This is, perhaps, in contrast with the British characteristic to consider that things are not what they are, but as they seem. And so, perhaps I should not have been surprised at the answer I received to my question when I addressed it to one of Her Majesty's most devoted and loyal privy councillors. I was having tea with the Rt. Hon. Enoch John Powell, MBE, MA, MP, until recently Defence Spokesman for Her Majesty's most loyal Opposition, in his Belgravia home. The question seemed to almost strike him dumb. Setting down the teapot with much deliberation, he stared at me fixedly and managed with incredulity in his tone to repeat my word. 'Function?' he asked, and then relieved the tension with the suggestion of a chuckle.

Finally, he replied: 'What a silly question. Nobody made it, so how could anybody know what its function is? The kingship is not a deliberate creation. It is not like the motor car. Perhaps more like intestines. Analytically, it can be viewed as having functions, but they are not the reasons for its existing. The monarchy is emotional, symbolical, totemistic and mystical.'

Well, there you are. With all due respect to Mr Powell, it seems to me that he did indeed categorize the monarchy's functions. For people have emotional, symbolical, totemistic and mystical needs, and the monarchy's function is to serve them. I would like to describe how I think these functions work, because I have been surprised to note how widespread seem to be British misconceptions about their monarchy and its importance. I think they need to understand it clearly, the better to cherish it. According to opinion polls, it appears that about 72 per cent of the British people think that the monarchy possesses some element of real and active political power. They are wrong. It

I

also appears that about 30 per cent of the British people, I imagine Enoch Powell among them, think the monarch is selected by divine intervention. However mystically satisfying that may be, it strikes me as patent nonsense. Or to put it another way, I would concede that the monarch is selected by divine intervention in the same way and in the same amount as you and I are for our respective functions.

But most startling to an American visitor is the discovery that about a sixth of the British people think they would like to see the monarchy abolished. I say they think this, but I doubt if they have thought it out. Most of this group count themselves members of the Labour party, no doubt Old Socialists, in spirit if not in age, whose ideas have become the most tired and reactionary on the British political scene. In their egalitarian zeal, they would like to whack off the top of the social pyramid, leaving only a flat bed of stones, inert and directionless. What glory would the Egyptian Pharaohs have found in tombs like that? No, structure is dominated by its topmost forms, and a better, more English, architectural metaphor would be to speak of the arch, and the monarchy as its keystone.

Now, I am not one of those Americans who envies the British monarchy, and secretly wishes we had it for ourselves. Those who feel that are looking backward, and are failing to take advantage of the joys and pride which their country offers. Despite our casting off of the British crown, we have in the United States our full structure of institutions, which flow from the ideas of Christian brotherhood and puritan self-help, from the object of the Constitution, and from its personification in the presidency.

All societies depend for their stability and smooth working order on certain institutions which they adopt in unique combination to suit their particular needs. When the combination is somehow altered, the balance must be restored, or trouble ensues. The British monarchy has been for too long a part of the British combination of institutions, and around it all the others have grown in dependent juxtaposition, for it to be susceptible of replacement without trauma. And it is uniquely suited to the British character.

Since appearances are so important to that character, so is the symbolic function of the monarchy. It is the legitimizing authority, not just of ministers and laws and other specifics, but of the nationhood. It is the fundamental cement. Sociology Professor Edward Shils of Chicago and Cambridge, a non-monarchist, defined for me the relevant paradox of this. 'The monarchy,' he said, 'appears anomalous. It appears to have no particular task. The method of succession makes it appear inappropriate. But society needs something which appears sacred, something to symbolize the system of order.' Something, indeed, which commands, in Walter Bagehot's phrase of a century ago, 'credulous obedience'. Here the royal myth functions as political fact. It draws prestige and solidarity of respect away from the prime minister. While Americans tend to think of this as a bad thing, the love felt for the monarch reduces the intensity of political hatreds. It provides an umbrella under which a prime minister has the freedom to function confidently with undisguised partisanship, less fettered by requirements of national consensus.

The monarchy is a totem in which the British see themselves joined together, through which they share a pride in their heritage, and by which they control their many fractious tendencies. The British character has been variously described as illogical, class-conscious and deferent, and the monarchy embodies these qualities. The British character has been further described as violent, immoral, insecure, lacking self-confidence, and overbearing, and the monarchy protects it against extreme maladjustment in these respects. Prince Philip has said, 'One of the things about the monarchy and its place – and one of the great weaknesses in a sense – is that it has to be all things to all people.' The weakness is that it must reflect rather than initiate. But the strength is that it is recognized by all, identified with, seen as the totem. In short, it has position, and to the British that is a lot. In British life, position is not easily challenged or aspired to. In America, an oft-repeated article of faith is that 'any man can be president'. And many considered as proof of this proposition the accession to the presidency of Harry S. Truman. It is a concept which reflects the American tradition of free-wheeling individual action. In Britain, contrary, perhaps, to Professor Shils, it seems appropriate that no man or woman can be king or queen unless he or she has been so predestined.

The illogical, the arbitrary and the sacred in the monarchy all contribute to its mysticism, and indeed it may one day take its stand on its mystical significance as the living nation. Enoch

Powell made the analogy of the Athenians returning to their demolished city 'to find, alive and flourishing in the midst of the blackened ruins, the sacred olive tree, the native symbol of their country'. So, he suggests, might Britain, in the days of vanished empire, regard her royal talisman. In a recent article entitled, 'Where politicians must take the lead', Deputy Tory Leader Reginald Maudling concluded that 'first we must rekindle our sense of true pride'. In my two years in Britain, I have seen little evidence that politicians are likely to accomplish this, but it is still possible that the monarchy could make a contribution.

Indeed the monarchy is an emotional thing. Just as the Queen is officially Defender of the Faith, so also can she be unofficially defender of the pride, a protective mechanism for the national self-confidence. It is a part of the British character to be easily embarrassed, and to seek to avoid embarrassment either by panicking or by doing nothing. No foreigner can fault the British for their Queen: he can only look up to her.

The deepest childhood emotion is parental love, and in a real psychological way the unruly public, childlike, looks to the monarch as a parent figure. Just as children need to feel that their parents are respected outside the family, so the monarch enjoys respect from abroad. Children may envy parents, and feel rebellious toward them, but they do not depose them.

Though hopefully a strength forever, yet the British monarchy is a fragile thing. It is the most delicate flower of its sceptered isle. Like a spider's web, its pattern is formed from delicate strands, whose structure is vital to the nourishment of its creator. The weaknesses of the monarchy are not of what it is, but of what it does; most of the serious criticism which is made of it in Britain is of its behaviour, not of its condition. The crown speaks – and offends. Or it does not speak – and is remote. The crown sticks to channels and protocol – and seems stuffy. Or it reaches out to the people – and makes enemies. It is a victim of the non-royal social hierarchy, which demands that attention be given to it in proper precedence.

The behaviour of the crown partly depends on the personality of its possessor, of course. But it is also something which the Palace carefully programmes and elaborately orchestrates. The orchestration seems to be informed by some sense of historical cyclicity. Thus is appears that the reign of Elizabeth II has so far been characterized by a remoteness and conservativeness unnatural for its time. It is as if the Queen were still paying penance for the mis-behaviour of her uncle, Edward, Duke of Windsor, when he made so bold to marry, not only a divorced woman, but, perish the thought, an American at that. I think the time has come for the Palace to ask itself how long the crown can be made to atone for such a sin. And it should ask itself unto what generation the daughters should be punished for the sins of the fathers. The Queen was brought up with interests which are too narrow, and habits which are too rigidified for this era of radical change. A person whose only real loves are horseback riding and horse racing is not easy for most people in this day and age to identify with. I understand the Queen herself has been heard to ask in exasperation when confronted with men of learning, 'Why didn't they educate me?'

It is a time of exploding knowledge, and the monarch is in constant contact with people who are engaged in that knowledge. It is time that he or she be able to contend, or at least to entertain at a level of some sophistication. Some progress has been made with the education of Prince Charles, who is at least attending Trinity College, Cambridge, under conditions less segregated than his grandfather George VI and great-great-grandfather Edward VII were able to enjoy. But why does the Palace have to orchestrate it, down to the selection of a balanced cross-section of other boys in the Prince's entry? One of those boys said he would have given anything not to be one of the chosen luckies. Thus are artificial attitudes provoked. The Palace should leave more to chance. This may risk some dangers to the royal mystery. But mystery must be balanced with relevance.

While the monarchy should set an example, it cannot set fashion, lest it be caught, high and dry, sporting a *passé* fad. But in reflecting fashion, it must never be too far behind. I once asked a friend of mine who runs a small company how he decided when to raise prices. His answer was, 'As soon as the big boys do, and be damn' sure I don't miss it by more than twenty-four hours.' I fear that the monarchy has fallen more than twenty-four hours behind fashion, and there has been no better recent example of this than the case of the Earl of Harewood. It became momentarily embarrassing for the Queen to be confronted with granting approval to the remarriage of her divorced relative, he who had been living in sin with his intended and their three-year-old love-child. This incident should never have happened because divorce is no longer unfashionable, and the Palace should have long since required that Harewood obtain his divorce. The Queen was placed in the position of failing to set example, because she had failed to keep up with fashion.

Granted that this image-making is a role which royalty performs, and that it takes two, a player and an audience, to make a role. The British public, as audience, certainly has its faults as well. The thing is a two-way street, and the right balance of familiarity should be sought. If the public loves their royalty, as they claim, they should be more accepting and less snickering. After all, in the family, acceptance is practically the definition of a loved one: I am reminded of Robert Frost's classic line, 'home is where, when you have to go there, they have to take you in'. Since it is so important for monarchy to be visible, the public should help to make that visibility more natural. The character trait which royalty cannot help the British with is their cruelty toward royalty. The people should recognize royalty as human like themselves. The boy in the Trinity College entry should recognize that the Prince has more problems than he does, and should not plead with sheepish helplessness, 'What can I say to him?' And if someone who has once been a guest at Buckingham Palace gets arrested for speeding, the press should not undertake to make that an occasion to embarrass the Royal Family.

The public may be the child, but this is a complex world, in which children must learn to grow up quickly. The British people have in their monarchy a prize possession, which they must nourish carefully in order to keep it strong. For her part, the Queen, at forty-three, can look forward to more than a score, perhaps even two score, more years to reign. Accompanied by her remarkably able husband, she can grow to ever greater usefulness to her subjects, and, as a parent figure, the passing years will make her less the girl and more the mother. The monarchy will inevitably change with the times, but the trick for all concerned will be to know which direction it should take, and to help it on its way.

COLIN MACINNES

Colin MacInnes was born in London on August 20 1914, and was brought up in Australia. He began writing after he left the army in 1945, at first chiefly radio scripts for the BBC of which he did about 1500. He has contributed essays mostly on the contemporary social scene to such journals as *The Times*, the *Guardian*, the *Sunday Times* and the *Observer*: among weeklies and monthlies, chiefly to *Twentieth Century* and *Encounter*: also to the *Spectator*, *Queen*, *New Left Review*, *Saltire Review* and the *Jewish Chronicle* and overseas to *Partisan Review* and *Cahier des Saisons*.

PUBLICATIONS

To the Victors the Spoils (1950), a chronicle of army occupation life in Germany; *June in her Spring* (1952), a poetic tragedy of adolescent love in the Australian bush; *City of Spades* (1957), an account of the African and West Indian immigration into England; *Absolute Beginners* (1959), a prose poem and a social criticism of London teenage life; *Mr Love and Mr Justice* (1960), a morality about the worlds of the police force and the ponces; *England, Half English* (1961), a selection of the essays described above with new material about English social and literary life; *All Day Saturday* (1966), which evokes a pre-war Australia far from the excursions into the London of his recent work; and *Sweet Saturday Night*, published in 1967, a social history of the English music hall.

OUR OWN KINGS

COLIN MACINNES

The chief obstacle to writing coherently about the monarchy is that even today you cannot be really sure exactly what you are allowed to say. I am, like all of us, one of the Queen's subjects, and to her I owe allegiance. So if I write, as I shall later, that I am at heart a republican, and try to explain why, am I not committing treason? But as I love my country, and have never consciously betrayed it, how can I feel treasonable in saying that I wish England were other than a monarchy? It is indeed remarkable, when one comes to think of it, that the monarchy is almost the only serious subject about which, in our country, we hesitate to express ourselves with total candour.

If I am not being fanciful in thinking this impediment to truth is real, it is perhaps an indication that we *do* all consider the monarchy an important theme; for on what other topic does this auto-censorship exist? It has always struck me, for example, that the convention whereby the question of monarchy is, by common consent, 'taken out of politics' – indeed, hardly discussed publicly at all – is a curious and revealing one. One might, of course, conclude that this consented silence reveals a feeling that the subject is unimportant or, alternatively, that almost everyone so agrees about it that discussion of it would be pointless – like debating the weather, or the phases of the moon. But surely, this *is* an important subject; surely the political structure within which one lives is of immense importance in any society that claims to be in some measure free and democratic. And if it is not discussed, this would seem to me to be because we do not see the political and social importance of the monarchy or, if we do, we are really a bit scared to speak candidly about it.

But the paradox is that, in another sense, everyone – or almost everyone – certainly is interested in the monarchy! For otherwise, why would there be those acres, those square miles, of text and photographs devoted to the subject? Yet why also, in those countless acres, should one so rarely see any discussion of the real nature of the monarchy considered not as something merely picturesque, but as an institution that, indirectly, affects all our lives?

I do not think there can be any doubt that the vast majority of my fellow-countrymen approve of, or at all events accept, the monarchy. And if they are reluctant to talk about it at all in a serious way, this may also be because they feel something like, 'Well, most of us agree about *that*, even if we disagree about everything else, so for heaven's sake stop being a nuisance, rocking the boat, and raising the question of what the monarchy really *means*.'

The next difficulty in criticizing the monarchy as an institution is that one may also appear to be criticizing the actual monarchs who have occupied the throne. Now certainly, before the reign of Queen Victoria, there were some very odd monarchs indeed, but she and her descendants (with one exception) have surely been unusually good as human beings and at their horribly difficult task – above all, if one compares their conduct with that of the incompetents and near-lunatics which other nations, when they had kings, had to put up with. Of Queen Victoria, whom one must rightly regard as the founder of the tradition whereby the monarch was loved and respected instead of being feared and loathed, it is impossible to speak with sufficient admiration. That she had weaknesses we all know, but even these were very 'human' ones, and her qualities are so formidable that one reaches for superlatives of praise. It has always seemed to me that the most remarkable quality of this thoroughly remarkable woman lay in her choice of a husband. Prince Albert has often had a bad press in England, and perhaps still has to some extent in the folk memory, yet surely he was a quite unusually good and talented man; and in choosing him and loving him so devotedly, the Queen showed rare wisdom from her earliest youth. And when, in later years, she chose as confidential servants a tipsy Scotch bully and a somewhat weird Hindu, is this not sympathetic in revealing that her dignity, despite raised eyebrows and titters behind fans, was unassailable?

King Edward VII is often mocked for his understandable weaknesses of the flesh, and his fussing over medals and ceremonial. Though not such a prodigious figure as his mother –

how could he have possibly been that? – his relentless sense of duty, and sympathy for foreign peoples are most attractive. So in particular was his welcoming of English Jews into English society, and the concern he and all his family felt for 'subject peoples'. They were, of course, imperialists; but they were not racialists, as so many inferior imperialists became, and at a time when the English seemed determined to murder the Irish (or as many of them as possible), the English monarchy stood up for them as far as it was able (which was not, of course, far enough). It is significant, also, that the 'common people' liked King Edward. And though it may be true 'the people', are sometimes taken in by demagogues – Horatio Bottomley springs inevitably to mind – they can also be shrewd and realistic in their instinctive judgements of the great.

For King George V the popular affection grew, in the end, to be even greater, and it was even more deserved; and surely the most recalcitrant republican could not fail to see in him a man who, being placed where he was by destiny, behaved extremely well. Although he was considered by some to be, despite his qualities, a dull dog, Sir Harold Nicolson has rightly reminded us that in three fields of knowledge, shooting, yachting and philately, he was an expert of international stature. These may seem trivial forms of expertise to the unthinking; but to me, at any rate, who could not hit an elephant, sail a boat on the Round Pond, or distinguish an Antigua Penny Puce from an Insurance stamp, they are remarkable. And surely, any man who is really versed in even one branch of knowledge is likely to understand better those he does not know – or, at any rate, realize he does *not* understand them, and be willing to learn.

King Edward VIII, in spite of his charms, broke this family spell of virtue chiefly because he seems never to have grasped what, in his position, he could do, and could not. But in his brother, George VI, an admirable figure reappeared – characterized again by that same gift possessed by Queen Victoria of choosing an outstanding consort. Nor can there be any doubt that our present sovereign is worthy of the achievements of her forebears. The criticisms that were made of her some years ago, by Mr Muggeridge and others, scarcely dealt with the profounder question of the value of the monarchy as such, but concentrated chiefly on personal qualities in the Queen that happened to displease them. Two strange strictures were of her accent, and her love for, and knowledge of, horses. Well, well, well! Since everyone in England has an accent of some kind or another (though everyone seems also to believe that only *he* has no accent), to single out any one kind of speech for scorn is the height of pretension and small-mindedness. And why are many English publicists so convinced that to know and ride horses is somehow a disgrace? I was reared in Australia, where no one would think this . . . for to ride a horse is far more difficult than to drive a car, and a knowledge of horses is at least a form of the direct contact with animal life so many city-dwellers disastrously lack. A horseman needs patience, skill, and courage – all attractive virtues. I do not know if the Prime Minister can ride a horse, but if he could, I might distrust him a bit less.

If all this is so, the critic of monarchy must concede that, so far as personal qualities go, for a century and a half the English monarchy has been exceptionally successful.

Yet another difficulty of writing without admiration of the monarchy as an institution is that whoever does so must appear to be – and doubtless often is – a vulgar fellow: one who delights in cocking a snook at all authority, and who assails a lofty institution simply because it sees him – if it notices him at all – as a self-important nobody who, even in a republic, would be recognized as such. Nor can it be denied that in anyone who declares himself hostile to the monarchy, there may be a strong element of inverted snobbery. Do most citizens take pleasure – or, at any rate, not mind – when the National Anthem is played at a theatrical performance? Then let me be the one who draws attention to himself by hastening to the exit, manifesting superior disapproval! Do simple people gloat over regal photographs? Let me be he who sneers at them for doing so!

That this inverted snobbery exists among many – if not all – of those who denigrate the monarchy is, I think, undeniable. Persons not invited to tea by dukes as a rule speak ill of dukes, yet would readily accept the invitation if it came; or worse still would refuse, then boast of that refusal. Speaking personally, I would certainly be delighted to see the inside of Buckingham Palace. Who wouldn't be, for clearly it houses one of the most unusual families in the world? Yet equally, I would be delighted to visit other inaccessible strongholds – the Vatican, the Kremlin, Muhammad Ali's training camp or, for that matter, a conclave of the Mafia syndicate in America. It is natural to be curious about places and persons so rare and esoteric; but I do not think that necessarily proves one secretly admires them or is critical of them because of envy.

To explain what the objections to a monarchy seem to me to be, I shall resume the chief arguments advanced in its favour, then try to refute them:

1. *Myth: To ensure their social and political cohesion, all peoples need a mythology which is generally accepted and believed; and in England, this myth is enshrined in the English monarchy.* That such a myth is indeed important can be seen by reflecting on the histories of peoples who have long survived. Thus the Jews, most ancient of peoples, have as their underlying myth the pact of their ancestors with Jehovah. The Romans had household gods, and even Caesars were included in their pantheon. The Russians have the myth of Holy Russia – a force, as the war showed, more potent than the recent mythologies of communism. The Americans have their Founding Fathers and an almost sacred Constitution promising life, liberty, and the pursuit of happiness (without, of course, keeping this promise – but that does not detract from the force of a believed myth). To read President de Gaulle, it is clear his conception of *La France* is one which the French Revolution merely altered in form, not in substance.

But if we examine these potent myths, we will see the notion of monarchy was not essential to them. One of these peoples, the Americans, never had kings at all, and though all the others did, once kings had vanished – or before they had even existed – the myth by no means lost its cohesive force.

Is it only in England, then, that a national myth must of necessity be personified by a monarchy? Even the English have, in moments of crisis, not always believed this. Our civil war is so distant now that it is hard to realize that 300 years ago, our ancestors – or many of them – questioned this assumption in the most radical manner. And even when, on later occasions, the monarchy was not questioned but the monarch was, the English had little hesitation in ridding themselves of an individual king. This happened to James II, and it is perhaps relevant to remember that it also happened in the lifetimes of many of us when Edward VIII, so lauded in his youth, was ruthlessly expelled by an almost universal will.

Indeed, unless one supposes that we English (which ambiguous term I use throughout to include the Celtic tribes) are entirely different from anyone else in the world, it is surely evident that a national or patriotic myth can exist whatever the form of government may be.

2. *Tradition: a monarchy enshrines and embodies the traditional virtues of the nation.* The key here is what is meant by 'tradition'. So often, and particularly in our country, this word is used to mean not that wisdom by which the present can learn from the past, but a sterile worship of the past itself – and a past often misunderstood, at that. Thus, to take minor but characteristic examples, an estate agent will describe as 'traditional' an imitation Tudor villa built today. A musician will speak of 'trad jazz' when he is imitating, and not evolving from, the styles of sixty years ago. Sir Winston Churchill had – as of so many things – a better understanding of what tradition really means. For it is related that when an admiral questioned an order on the grounds that its execution would be 'contrary to the finest traditions of the British navy', the P.M., eyeing him balefully, declared, 'The traditions of the British Navy are rum, sodomy and the lash'.

That the monarchy is 'traditional' in the sense of being old, is undeniable. But is it traditional in the vital sense of helping our country to move with the times, adapt itself to change, confront the dilemmas of a harrassing, fast-evolving world? For this, I see no evidence at all; rather the contrary, in fact. For it seems to me that if, alone among major powers except for Japan, we still adhere tenaciously to this institution, it is yet another direful proof we still live in the past, and cling to lost glories no one cherishes, or even recognizes, save for ourselves.

3. *All nations must have a head of state; and a monarch is more dignified – a fitter symbol – than any president.* The first part of this proposition seems to me correct, and the second quite untrue. If the head of state be also its chief executive (as in America or France), the question scarcely arises as our monarch

no longer has these powers. If the head of state is purely decorative (as in India or Russia), almost any loyal and presentable old boy can adequately fill the role.

4. *As its head, our monarch helps to preserve the Commonwealth.* This is believed to some extent in England, a little in Australia, a very little in Canada – but nowhere else, so far as I can discover from enquiry among citizens of other Commonwealth countries. That a visit from the Queen to some part of the Commonwealth may be welcomed is still probably true – but so would one from Mrs Jaqueline Kennedy or, for that matter, Mrs Elizabeth Burton. The value – the 'credibility', as the jargon goes – of these visits has in any case been greatly devalued in the past fifteen years. Even the Australians thought we were beginning to overdo it, and a visit by the Queen to Canada can now provoke more disunity than harmony.

In reality, Commonwealth citizens and governments have long seen the empty title 'Head of the Commonwealth' for what it is: a last ditch claim of English neo-Imperialism, trying to preserve an illusion of past splendours and authority that have vanished. If the Commonwealth exists in any real sense at all – which is increasingly doubtful – it does so only in terms of politics, trade and cultural exchange.

Let us now consider some positive disadvantages of a monarchy which are usually neglected by those who seek to sustain it.

The first arises from the fiction that a constitutional monarchy has no positive political powers. It can advise, warn, and so forth, but it cannot act. And if it cannot act, it no longer presents, as it did in the past, any danger to democratic government. But a moment's reflection should surely convince us that the notion that modern English monarchy has no *political* power is a complete fable.

First of all, because anyone like a monarch who has the contacts with, and the information about, all the most important personalities and acts within the nation possesses, by this very fact, enormous potential powers. It is probably correct to say that no one – no single other man or woman in the country – knows as much about who is who, and who is doing what, as does the monarch. This knowledge can be used or misused, but to deny it constitutes effective political power is to reject everybody's experience of how any joint human endeavour really works.

The next power arises from the monarch's capacity to act, almost as an individual, in certain moments of crisis. A study of the lives of all the monarchs mentioned earlier proves that in, for example, the matter of selecting prime ministers, or dissolving parliament, in abnormal moments of crisis the decision, whatever the conventions may be, can in the last resort be that of the monarch personally.

In time of war this political power could manifestly become crucial. Let us suppose ourselves invaded, and that the monarch either stays to struggle with his people (as did the Danish King in World War II), or continues the battle overseas (as did, among others, the Norwegian). Either decision may ultimately be the better ... and again, the decision to go or stay might be removed from the monarch's choice by the sudden march of events. Yet, clearly, whatever decision the monarch made, or was forced to make, could be politically vital. And if it be said that the same would apply to a non-monarchical head of state, this would not be so, because none of the mythological aura surrounds a president as it does a king. In such an event – which, given the state of the world, we should surely at least envisage – a monarch's posture would become of the greatest political importance.

In this connection, we might recall that even in a quite minor crisis, a monarch can have a divisive, rather than a stablizing, influence. The abdication of King Edward VIII is perhaps the greatest non-event in history. Judged objectively, it was of no consequence whatever. But judged in terms of the pained and violent emotions it aroused in the nation, we can see that the myth of monarchy confers of any monarch a disturbing power to create a national crisis out of what is, in effect, a merely personal one.

We must also consider what the political views of any individual monarch might happen to be. The convention, of course, is that the monarchy is a-political – 'above politics', as they say. This is clearly nonsense. In the first place, there is no human being on earth who does not hold political views of some kind, for even when these are not consciously articulated, and even when a person may declare himself to be 'non-political' his views, and consequently actions, must of necessity conform to one or another set of political ideas.

To this, a constitutional monarch is no exception. And indeed, the biographies of all our monarchs prove that their political ideas were often most decided. This is not to deny that they could be relatively objective about the rival claims of various parties, provided these claims fell broadly within a political pattern of which they on the whole approved. Thus George V, for instance, was helpful to the first Labour governments, once he was convinced that they were – as indeed they were and still are – basically nationalist and not socialist in any radical way.

But can one not conceive a situation in which a majority of our countrymen might indeed become radically socialist, and wish to alter the economic situation of our nation? In which they might become not only anti-capitalist, but even anti-monarchical? However unlikely this may at present seem – and indeed is – can anyone imagine that a monarchy, itself 'traditional' and itself possessed of enormous wealth, could view such a movement of opinion, if it sought power, with 'non-political' objectivity?

The fact, surely, is that a monarchy, as it is hereditary, is by essence a conservative institution, and because of its possessions, a capitalist one. Since the vast majority of our people in whatever party are equally conservative and wedded to capitalism (whether they call themselves Conservative, Labour or whatever), the fiction of the monarchy being 'non-political' can be maintained without great strain. But to suggest that our constitutional monarchy is by its nature 'non-political' is absurd.

A further critique of monarchy may be made in terms not of its political, but of its social consequences. It is, I think, generally admitted that English class hierarchies are more rigid than in most countries, despite the greater mobility between classes that has arisen in the past 150 years. Of course, there is no country in the world where class structures do not exist – for example, since the October revolution, communist nations have developed these with remarkable rapidity. It is also undeniable that many Englishmen and women, even of the working class, do tacitly accept, and even approve of, these class divisions. (One of the reasons for working-class acceptance of the higher orders is not, as these fondly imagine, because the workers admire them or are deceived by their pretensions, but because it is often simpler to manipulate pretensions from the lower rank. This is how, in the Army, all sergeants learn to use most officers, letting these officers imagine that they are manipulating the NCOs.) But if one may feel that the more classless a society is, the healthier it is, these class divisions seem sterile, retrogressive. And by 'class' I do not mean distinctions of inherent talent and even earnings, which are manifestly legitimate, but arbitrary divisions depending largely not on natural talent but on inherited social position and its consequent educational advantages.

Now clearly, a society in which the apex of the social pyramid is hereditary, will offer less possibility of social mobility than any other. An American may dream of becoming president, a Russian first secretary, and a priest, pope; but no Englishman can dream of becoming king. The monarchy thus acts, by its very existence, as a symbol, a manifest proof, that what you were born, you should remain. And though Englishmen and women have risen by their talents to the highest spheres, this potent national myth encourages the notion of our society being basically, by its very nature, hierarchically established.

All societies reward those deemed worthy of social praise with badges of social merit, as well as with material rewards. The Soviet Union has its Heroes, the French republic its Legionaries of Honour, and even America its Honorables and civilian badges of distinction. But in England, thanks to the existence of a monarchy, these awards reach extraordinary proportions. And what is significant is that, because they consist not so much of national as of regal embellishments of infinite variety, this has the consequence of wedding the recipients not only to the society that honours them, but to the 'traditional' structure of the society.

This process, which most take for granted as being in the nature of things, is subtle and pervasive in its effects. The elder radical, since there is no senate, has the choice between political oblivion or becoming a life peer – and hence, by definition, no longer radical at all (though he would, of course, deny this). The final accolade of any institution is to become 'royal', and thus committed to a conservative conception of society. What greater honour could the Sadlers Wells ballet company have had than to be known by their own name which they themselves had made internationally famous by their art? But no, they must become the Royal Ballet. The final absurdity is reached when regiments of the Army (not itself 'royal', surprisingly, unlike its sister services) became 'royal' too: imagine the gratification of a military copper when his corps is thus ennobled! An ancilliary curiosity of this social habit is the degree to which it encourages the illustrious of our land perpetually to be dressing up, like children at a charade. The English elders, who say they despise display, and are infinitely scornful of the dress fantasies of the young, are given to donning fancy dress, almost always of a 'regal' nature, to a really astonishing degree. An American president, or judge, or senator, dresses like a man: in our own land, they dress up like popinjays. This may be great fun, but it can be questioned if it really enhances any natural dignity these persons may possess; and does not, on the contrary, encourage them to fall still deeper into the world of make-believe in which our country at present fatally dwells.

The English monarch is also head of the English church, which is established. In a nation which is, at best, latently Christian only and, where fervently so, mostly among sects deemed 'nonconformist', this regal patronage of a particular faith has the weird effect of making the mass of the population *ad hoc* Anglicans, even when they manifestly are not. I recall, in the Army, that those who did not declare themselves to be Roman Catholics, or Protestant dissenters of some species (known courteously, in the Army, as 'odds and sods'), were dubbed automatically 'C of E'. That this description may have encouraged any of them who, not being conscious Anglicans, were so defined, to respect either the Church of England or Christianity itself, I greatly doubt. But since the monarch was the head of the Anglican church, it seemed disloyal to declare themselves what most of them in fact were, which is unbelievers or, at best, hearty doubters.

Then what, the hostile reader may be thinking, does all this amount to? You have said your disrespectful piece . . . but what do you want to *do*? Chop off the monarch's head, and elect some ghastly politician president? And if you do want this, do you really imagine anyone of substance agrees with you?

As I have said, I think the vast majority of my countrymen accept, or acquiesce in, the existence of a monarchy, so that I have no illusions as to the answer to the last question I have posed myself. As for chopping off anyone's head, even the Russians do not do that now (or don't do it in public view), and if it does not sound presumptuous to say so, I feel no individual animosity whatever to the royal family – rather the contrary, in fact, as they seem to me better human beings than most of us. I just wish they would fade away, together with their castles and picture collections and fortunes, into a dignified retirement. As to an elected head of state, are we English really incapable of finding *anyone* we trust to fulfil this function in what we believe to be a democracy?

All foreign observers have noticed, and we have even begun to realize it ourselves, that we live, as a nation, in a world of daydream. In a century, we have fallen from power to relative insignificance, from immense riches to near bankruptcy. Our survival depends on a vigorous and most realistic (and most painful) readaptation of ourselves to what, in the modern world, we are and can be.

In this endeavour, some see the monarchy as a helpful force, creating stability, binding us together as we lick our wounds and prepare to fight again. I am bound to say I see it as having a totally opposite effect: of preserving dangerous illusions of grandeur, and of being one factor among many that inhibits national revival.

The real English myth we should cherish, and which can sustain us, is not enshrined in an archaic monarchical survival. It exists in what is essential to us, and which kings have never formed: our blend of races, our created language, our scientific, commercial and artistic skills, our faith. 'God save the King' is a splendid motto; 'God save ourselves', a real one.

'The Express is a bloody awful newspaper,' said the Duke. 'Ah, well,' said Lord B., as they trotted him off to the Tower, 'at least he takes it or he wouldn't know it was a bloody awful newspaper.'

COMPTON MACKENZIE

Sir Compton Mackenzie was born at West Hartlepool in 1883. He was educated at St Paul's School and Magdalen College, Oxford. In World War I he served with the RND in the Dardenelles Expedition and was invalided in September, 1915. As Captain RM he was Military Control Officer in Athens in 1916. In 1917 he was Director of the Aegean Intelligence Service. He was awarded the OBE and Legion of Honour. He was Rector of Glasgow University from 1931 to 1934. He is C.Lit., Hon.LL.D., Hon.R.S.A. and Knight Commander of the Phoenix (Greece). He has published over 100 books including eight Octaves of *My Life and Times* and *The Windsor Tapestry*.

THE SCOTTISH POINT OF VIEW

COMPTON MACKENZIE

Thirty-five years ago the University of Glasgow of which I was Rector at the time gave the honorary degree of LL D to their Royal Highnesses the Duke and Duchess of York. At the lunch which followed the ceremony I was seated next to the Duchess and I recall her asking me what I thought was the feeling in Scotland for the monarchy. It was a way of asking more particularly what was the feeling of what was then called the National Party of Scotland for the monarchy. I replied that whatever happened Scotland would remain faithful to the Crown and that if the Union were dissolved any independent Scotland would be independent under the Crown as it was when James I and VI ascended the throne of Great Britain. I added that neither Cunninghame Graham nor myself would support any republican notions for independence; Scotland would never tolerate a republic.

I ask myself if I could give as confident an answer today were I asked the same question. As I write these words the Scottish National Party has just won from Labour what seemed as safe a seat as Labour ever held. Tories, Liberals and Socialists alike are anxiously maintaining that the election of Mrs Winifred Ewing is merely the expression of a temporary irritation with the economic policy of the Government now in power. Writing as one who for forty years has been arguing in favour of a dissolution of the Union I can assert that for the first time during those forty years I am able to imagine such a dissolution's being achieved in my lifetime. That being so I am passionately anxious that the monarchy will not be misled by its advisers into appearing to disregard the rising tide.

When King Edward VII ascended the throne in 1901 there was a protest signed by some hundred thousand Scots against his failure to be called Edward VII and I. But in 1901 the Scots still had a British Empire of which they fancied they were the mainstay. There were some who hoped for a measure of home rule but the idea of dissolving the Union hardly existed. When our present Queen ascended the throne half a century later her advisers ignored Scottish sentiment and she was proclaimed Queen as Elizabeth II; she was in fact Elizabeth II and I. On top of that the Queen's short-sighted advisers wearing court monocles or bureaucratic spectacles were afraid of any competition with the coronation in London except overseas in the Commonwealth. To receive the crown of Scotland the Queen carried a handbag over her arm and did not wear coronation robes. If, which God forbid, Scotland should become a republic, those myopic advisers down in London will have contributed to such a disaster.

One of the paradoxes of history is that when the Irish embarrassed the English most successfully they were always led by a Protestant and that when the Scots embarrassed the English most successfully they were always led by a Catholic. Yet a greater paradox than either is the fact that after the death of Edward the Confessor the English continued to be ruled for centuries in turn by Norman, French, Welsh, Scottish, Dutch and German monarchs. George III made much of being a true-born Briton, but the way in which he lost the American colonies was essentially Germanic.

The years of war with France throughout which the Scots were allies of the French were wars between dynasties rather than wars between nations. When the war in France ended, the Wars of the Roses carried on another dynastic struggle in England, which ceased when that sinister Tudor defeated Richard III at Bosworth.

I have fancied that when Shakespeare blackened the House of York to exalt the House of Lancaster he was offending his own conscience and that the great tragedies he wrote later were inspired by a desire to atone for his earlier surrender to expediency. I would go so far as to argue that Hamlet was as near as Shakespeare ever came to a portrait of himself.

What would Shakespeare have made of the Great Rebellion, if he had lived through it, and the martyrdom of King Charles the First for his belief in the divine right of kings? Shakespeare wrote in *Hamlet* of the divinity that hedged a king, but that belief must have received a shock when, partly through envy, Elizabeth sent Mary Queen of Scots to the scaffold. Elizabeth was haunted by the memory of Fotheringay to the end of her days, when her conscience drove her from bed to sit in a corner of the room, fearful of death's after-life.

Once the English had made the execution of a monarch legal it was inevitable that any monarch in future who was adjudged to have ruled against the will of his people was liable to execution. Yet in spite of the regicides a belief in the divine right of monarchy lasted. The average man who had endured the decade of the Protectorate was thankful for the Glorious Restoration. Nor did Charles II disappoint them. True, there was the Plague and the Fire of London, the imaginary Popish plot and an all too real Dutch fleet sailing up the Thames, but it was James II and VII who damaged the popular appeal of the monarchy after his brother had pleased the London mob by making an orange-girl from Drury Lane his mistress and their son a duke. 'I'm the Protestant whore,' she told the rioters; and they cheered her carriage on its way.

In his desire to make the position of Catholics easier James tried equally hard to lighten the tyranny of the Church of England over Protestant nonconformity. His attempts at religious toleration brought him into direct conflict with the Anglican bishops while at the same time he was supporting the Scottish bishops against the Covenanters. When the plot to bring in William of Orange as king to share the throne with James's daughter Mary succeeded, some of those bishops with whom James had been in conflict found it impossible to take the oath of allegiance to the usurper. Those non-jurors were not only courageous, they were also logical. Once the Anglican Church had accepted Henry VIII's claim to be its supreme head it was necessary to accept as an article of faith the divine right of kings. William's enterprise was financed by the gin-makers of Holland whom he repaid by giving gin a monopoly as an alcoholic spirit, with the deplorable results that Hogarth would depict half a century later.

Twenty-eight years after the Glorious Restoration the inglorious Revolution would destroy the hopes of Charles II and James II and VII of a *rapprochement* between England and France. Instead, England was committed to a foreign policy which would lead to the gradual aggrandizement of Prussia and ultimately to the German belief that it was the divine destiny of the Fatherland to rule the world.

The rebellions of the Fifteen, the Nineteen and the Forty-five should all be seen as expressions of Scottish resentment of the Union as much as of loyalty to the king over the water. Nevertheless, Prince Charles Edward's personal appeal was powerful. When he reached Paris after his adventures he was followed by a cheering crowd whenever he appeared in public. Louis XV began to ask himself whether if the Young Chevalier decided to claim the throne of France he would be supported by the people of France. The Stuarts still quartered the lilies in the royal arms, thus implying that they still claimed the throne.

When in the spring of 1748 the envoys of the belligerent powers met in Aix-la-Chapelle to discuss terms of peace, one of the proposed clauses was to guarantee the succession of the Crown of Great Britain to the House of Hanover. Prince Charles protested against this and when the preliminaries of peace were signed he was officially notified of the probability of his having to quit French territory. Yet, except with the Court and the Ministers, Charles remained the most popular figure in France and that popularity grew daily. He could not take a walk without being followed by an admiring crowd; his presence in the theatre diverted all attention from the play. Louis became more and more anxious about a popular rising and a threat to his own throne. He was determined to get Charles out of Paris.

Twelve hundred of the guards watched the approaches to the Opera House, and troops lined the streets from the Palais Royal to Vincennes. Even scaling-ladders were provided for an attack on the Prince's house. On the evening of December 11th, that disastrous date for royalty, Charles drove to the Opera House. The moment he alighted he was seized by several guards, disarmed and wound round with a quantity of pink ribbon. He was then carried to a coach and driven to the Château of Vincennes where he was imprisoned for several days. The French public were enraged when they heard of his treatment. The Dauphin himself protested to his father, and it is not too much to say that when Louis XV signed the decree for Charles's expulsion he signed at the same time the death warrant of the Bourbons. So the Prince was expelled to the Papal city of Avignon, but even there the Hanoverians thought he was a threat to them, and he was forced to leave Avignon and wander round Europe, his whole life thwarted.

One may fairly speculate that if Charles had succeeded to the throne of Great Britain there would have been no revolt of the American colonies and that if he had ascended the throne of France there would have been no French revolution. It is tragic that the two royal figures who were able to realize that democracy must soon assert itself were Charles Edward Stuart and Gustavus III of Sweden who would befriend Charles Edward in those sad days ahead. Charles was denied the opportunity to show how closely in touch as a king he would have been with popular feeling; Gustavus III was assassinated by those who dreaded the effect of his liberal ideas.

When the French followed the example set to them by the English of cutting off royal heads the English themselves were rightly outraged by the execution of Louis XVI and Marie Antoinette, but with their unequalled ability among nations to forget what was disagreeable or disgraceful in their own past they now supposed such an outrage was unimaginable in Great Britain.

There was no Restoration in France but human nature's feeling for monarchy was still lively enough to make Napoleon's achievement possible, and it could be argued that, however much other monarchs might look down on the *parvenu* French Empire, it was Napoleon who gave monarchy new life through the efforts of hereditary monarchs to destroy that Empire. This they certainly would never have succeeded in doing unless England in the words of Pitt had saved Europe by her example. The corruption of power would probably have been fatal to Napoleon's attempt to build a new Europe. Nevertheless, it is not too wild a speculation to ask whether, if at first Pitt had worked with Napoleon instead of against him, they might not have built between them a better Europe than the Europe built by the Peace of Vienna.

In Great Britain the Reform Act and the personally popular William IV safeguarded the monarchy, and the girl who on that morning in June received homage as Queen and as head of the Church of England was a fresh source of strength to that monarchy. It was inevitable as head of the Church of England that she would marry a German prince. Europe by now was divided between inbred Catholic royalty and inbred Protestant royalty, much the richest source of supply being Germany. It was a happy marriage and when the Prince Consort died his widowed Queen indulged herself in such a prolonged display of grief that as the years went by her subjects began to lose the personal affection which she had inspired when she came to the throne. During the seventies there were republican murmurings going around, one of the most audible being Joseph Chamberlain's. The Queen now made an effort to appear more often in public and by the time her golden jubilee was celebrated she was again a beloved and popular figure.

It was a pity that she did not abdicate in the following autumn. If the Prince of Wales could have become king in 1887, the decade of the nineties, instead of achieving nothing but ill-considered Imperial aggrandizement might have seen home rule for Ireland, votes for women, slum clearance on a vast scale and many social reforms. The Prince of Wales, who had shown himself genuinely anxious to help social reform, was denied any part in state affairs. He was left with little to do except amuse himself; as a result his love affairs became the gossip first of Mayfair, then of the suburbs, and at last even of the servants' hall, while his gambling and horse-racing excited the self-righteous sighs of the middle classes.

The Baccarat case of 1891, produced one of those disgusting vomits of self-righteousness to which the British public surrenders from time to time. When Sir William Gordon-Cumming was unsuccessful in securing a verdict in a libel action he brought against a family of *nouveaux riches* who had accused him of cheating at cards, the Prince of Wales was called as a witness.

Here is *The Times* on June 10th, White Rose Day:

'We are but expressing the universal feeling of millions of Englishmen and Englishwomen when we say that we profoundly regret that the Prince should have been mixed up, not only in this case, but in the social circumstances which prepared the way for it ... What does concern and indeed distress the public is the discovery that the Prince should have been at the baccarat table; that the game was apparently played to please him ... if the Prince of Wales is known to frequent certain circles and to eschew those with a greater claim upon the notice of royalty; if he is known to pursue on his private visits a certain round of questionable pleasures into which other people, perhaps young people, are often drawn against their will by mere complaisance, the serious public – who after all are the back-bone of England (!) regret and resent it.'

Here is the *Daily News,* the organ of nonconformity:

'The pity of it all is in the presence of the heir to the throne at the head of the baccarat table ... The Prince of Wales is bound to a pure, a simple, and a cleanly life as rigorously as if the obligation were set down in some constitutional pact ... Woe to the monarchy when it can no longer perform what may fairly be called its last surviving use.'

The rest of the London press was equally nauseating and the provincial and Scottish press as bad. The *Liverpool Courier:*

'It is surely an unedifying spectacle to see the future King of England officiating as "banker" at such a gambler's orgy.'

The *Nottingham Express:*

'The British Empire is humiliated, and the rest of civilization is pointing a finger at us.'

The *Dundee Advertiser:*

'The Prince of Wales is evidently not what, with such a destiny before him, he ought to be.'

Macaulay observed that there was no spectacle so ridiculous as the British public in one of its periodic fits of morality.

The Times would indulge in a contemptible fit of morality over the abdication of King Edward VIII but the British public on the whole abstained.

The Times indulged in another fit of morality at the time of the Profumo case and on that occasion the British public was equally absurd.

I wrote to the Editor from France:

'I wonder if you realize how turbid in the clear air of France appears this torrent of self-righteousness pouring down your columns.'

The letter was not printed for 'reasons of space' which added a final touch of humbug to the attitude of *The Times*.

For another ten years after the Baccarat case the Prince of Wales was kept out of any part in affairs of state but his popularity steadily increased. The public was shocked when Princess May married Prince George a year after her fiancé the Duke of Clarence died, but the public realized that Queen Victoria was responsible for this marriage, not the Prince of Wales, and Princess May soon become a very popular royal figure.

As Queen Victoria grew older and older she inevitably became more and more deeply revered, and her Diamond Jubilee almost made the public believe that she personally during her long reign had created the British Empire. On that windless silver-grey morning when the twentieth century was just a month old there could not have been many spectators of the Queen's funeral who had any doubts about the future of monarchy as those kings and princes rode behind that royal coffin.

I find that young people today look back to the Edwardian decade much as I when young looked back to the Regency. To them it seems a time when people knew how to live and life was much more exciting. Most of us who were young in that Edwardian decade did not feel that we were safely free from Victorianism until the Liberal victory in the General Election of 1906. King Edward himself played no part in that awakening. Where he did play an immensely important part was in the Entente Cordiale. It is the fashion among contemporary historians to attribute the Entente Cordiale to the foresight and diplomatic skill of the exhausted Tory government. What contemporary historians, like all economists contemporary and past, fail to grasp is the decisive influence of the human factor. All the skill of politicians and diplomats would have been wasted if King Edward had not been able to win the hearts of the French people, and those hearts were won by a monarch in a republic.

In 1904 the people of Great Britain were being tempted by Joseph Chamberlain into a belief that an alliance with Germany was the right policy for Great Britain. I recall being laughed at for writing in an editorial of the *Oxford Point of View* that the way to avoid a European war in the future was to confront the Triple Alliance with another Triple Alliance between France,

Russia and Great Britain. When I argued for this at a college debate I was heavily defeated. This was because the British have always suspected the Russian bear whatever the colour of his fur.

What King Edward VII did to promote the Entente Cordiale could only have been done by a monarch. No president or prime minister could have changed French suspicion of English perfidy.

When George V became king there was to some extent a return to Victorianism at court but whatever Germanic aspects of royalty were apparent vanished with the outbreak of the First World War. It was considered advisable for the British monarchy to dissociate itself completely from its German connections, and to stress this the royal house became Windsor. At the same time Teck became Cambridge and Battenberg Mountbatten.

In spite of the break-up of the German, Austrian and Russian empires and the exile or murder of their emperors the British Empire and the King-Emperor seemed secure. Sentiment in the dominions for monarchy was kept warm by the success with which the Prince of Wales was able to present himself as a democratic royal figure and suggest that the nineteenth century was a bygone age.

The Prince's accession to the throne was for some years beforehand regarded with apprehension by both Establishments. Establishment used to be the name for the Church of England until during this century it has become an inclusive word for all those who rule the country, either directly or indirectly.

King Edward VIII gave both Establishments their opportunity to disembarrass themselves of what they feared would be an unreliable pillar by proposing to marry an American divorcée. The operation of driving the King into abdication was performed with masterly humbug by Stanley Baldwin and with less skilfully concealed hostility by the Archbishop of Canterbury and the Editor of *The Times*.

The shock of the abdication was not so severe as it might have been if King George VI had not assumed with such courage and balance a burden he had never desired to carry.

For one thing monarchy should be grateful to the Duke of Windsor. His example as Prince of Wales made it possible for the Duke of Edinburgh to speak out as he does. He was the bridge between King George V and Prince Philip.

When after the Second World War more thrones collapsed

those which remained firm were unmistakably democratic monarchies. It is easier to be a democratic monarch in the comparative intimacy of Copenhagen or The Hague than to be Queen of Great Britain, Queen of Canada, Queen of Australia and even Queen of Malta. What should have impressed those who are asking whether our country requires a monarchy was the way a visit from the Queen to Malta in 1967 changed the atmosphere of the island at the time.

There is no threat to the monarchy at this moment; but the children of today, who are being brought up to take for granted what their parents had to keep on demonstrating, that Jack is as good as his master, may decide that monarchy is an expensive luxury. The sadly inadequate educational system of today, which believes that it is more important for a child to be taught some odds and ends of physics or chemistry than to be taught history, will intensify a belief already prevalent among the young that the past is unimportant.

The attack on heredity in which the Prime Minister is in the front line is largely due to what in the jargon of psychoanalysts used to be called an inferiority complex. It is ironical that, when our forebears are blamed for the weakness, folly and vice we inherit from them, their virtues are never supposed to owe anything except to ourselves. A politician who has the character and ability to become prime minister should be proud and grateful for this; he should not give the impression that he has an aching chip on his shoulder because he was not at Eton. It is clear that in due course the House of hereditary Lords will disappear and that its place will be taken by a House of life Lords. Will that be the first step toward an elective monarchy?

Such a monarchy would no doubt be chosen at first from the Royal Family but inevitably heredity would after a time be denounced as a handicap, and presently Tom, Dick or Harry could become president with no more power than a French president was allowed until General de Gaulle realized that a little more monarchy was necessary and rejuvenated France. The apparent inability of the British to appreciate his achievement is disquieting because it suggests a fear of monarchy, whether such monarchy be hereditary or not. The example set by dictators during this century is not encouraging but the power that corrupted them was inspired by its novelty. General de Gaulle avoided dictatorship; his inspiration was his country's past. He was wise enough to understand that whatever the external change in the condition of his time man remains what he was created. Woman may seem to have been changed by the conditions of today but it should be remembered that matriarchy preceded patriarchy and the course of man's immediate future will again be set by women. The fall of Scotland from independent nationhood was primarily due to the Scots following a man like John Knox instead of their queen and, like her son King James I and VI, allowing themselves to be captivated by what seemed the richer glitter of the English crown.

As I write these words there is a greater upsurge of Scottish nationalism than any since the Forty-five, and the most hopeful sign for the future is that the pioneer is a woman. At the same time we have a queen who is half Scottish, and if for no other reason I pray that if independence be regained such independence will be under the Crown.

But leave Scotland out of it. I believe that the only chance for Britain to survive the remainder of this century without becoming a dependency of the United States is to retain the monarchy.

When at the beginning of this century the progressive dons of Oxford succeeded in getting compulsory Greek abolished from Responsions I argued in print that such a surrender would prepare the way for the collapse of the British Empire; I did not expect that my prophecy would be fulfilled in my own lifetime. At school like so many other schoolboys I had groaned over the necessity to distinguish a present or past general from a present or past particular when wrestling with Greek conditional sentences, but the failure of most politicians to have had that elementary piece of logic drummed into their heads in childhood may have been one of the causes of the increasing political ineptitude which has characterized politics since politics became a more and more lucrative profession.

Even more injurious than the abandonment of Greek, which would inevitably lead as it now has to the abolition of Latin, is the pathetic belief of contemporary historians and economists that statistics cannot err. Carlyle once observed that history was the essence of innumerable biographies; at about the same time Emerson observed that there was properly no history, only biography. I must assume that the young are too often taught history today by teachers who did not learn in early youth the difference between the particular and the general.

Hereditary monarchy means that a human being carries in himself the known virtues and vices, the known follies and wisdom of his forefathers from the preceding centuries. Undoubtedly there is a growing inclination among the unripe fruits of egalitarianism to regard the monarchy as an expensive luxury of the Establishment, an anachronism in the brave new world of today. When those unripe fruits are more mature a couple of generations hence they will not be embittered by hereditary social advantages because equality will be taken for granted by then and will no longer feel it must assert itself. Whether that future monarchy will feel able to undertake the burden that grows heavier year by year is a question nobody without the inheritance of that burden could pretend to answer.

During the Second World War Winston Churchill became the symbol of Great Britain's will to survive. France was fortunate to have a man like de Gaulle able to guide her back to greatness by a limited monarchy instead of a dictatorship because he was the symbol of France's will to survive. In the equally difficult days before Great Britain (or what may be England and Scotland) let the monarchy remain as the symbol of the two countries' will to survive.

DERMOT MORRAH

Dermot Morrah was born in 1896 and educated at Winchester College. After active service as an officer of the Royal Engineers he returned to New College, Oxford, and, having taken a first in Modern History, was elected Fellow of All Souls in 1921. He resigned from the Home Civil Service to enter journalism and was for thirty years a leader-writer for *The Times;* on reaching the age limit of Printing House Square he transferred to the *Daily Telegraph*, retiring finally in 1967. This service overlapped with twenty-one years as editor of *The Round Table*.

He began to write on the monarchy in 1937, when *The Times* sent him to Westminster Abbey as its principal representative for the coronation of George VI. Since then he has been responsible for a series of popular books on royal topics, published in aid of King George's Jubilee Trust, and two more serious studies, *The Work of the Queen* (1958) and *To Be a King* (March, 1968), an account of the education of the Prince of Wales.

Mr Morrah was appointed by the Queen, shortly after her accession, to be Arundel Herald Extraordinary, and he is a Fellow of the Society of Antiquaries and a Freeman of London.

THE SOCIAL MONARCHY

DERMOT MORRAH

The great company of men and women who assemble annually at the Queen's invitation in her Palace of Westminster has claims to be considered the oldest social gathering in the world. The adjective 'social' is essential. Politically, parliament is a creation of yesterday, barely seven centuries old, younger than the Althing of Iceland or the Conclave that elects the Pope.

But the brilliant social function over which the Queen presided on Hallow-e'en of 1967 traces its origins far back beyond the oldest annals of the English race, beyond even their arrival in the British Isles. J. E. A. Jolliffe, the constitutional historian writes:

'... just within the shadow at which the records of English history fail stands the sacrificial king. The three high feasts of English heathendom were Winter's Day (November 7), Midwinter's Day (December 25), and Summer's Day (May 7). Under the Christian dispensation "thrice a year the king wore his crown. At Easter he wore it at Winchester, at Pentecost at Westminster, and at Midwinter at Gloucester", and there was feasting and entertainment of the king's faithful men.'

In feudal England it was natural to make these crown-wearings, the parties that brought together the king's faithful men to enjoy his hospitality, the occasions for consultation with them on the high business of the realm, consultations which by the thirteenth century had come to be called great parleys, or parliaments. And so the tradition, continuous from the remote pagan past, has been carried on to this day. It is observed only once a year instead of three times; but the essence of the occasion is the same. The Queen is at home to her guests. It is the most important party she ever gives, so she wears her best hat – the imperial state crown. The guests also – or at least the better-mannered of them – are dressed up to the nines. Although there is to be a parley (after the hostess has withdrawn), and she therefore receives them in her parlour, or parliament chamber, her invitations have been by no means confined to the accredited legislators who will take part in the discussions. She has her family with her – not only her husband and her son, who have or will have seats in the legislature, but her daughter, her sister and other near relations who are outside it.

The representatives of her brother sovereigns and heads of state, in the polychromatic plumage of the Diplomatic Corps, have places of honour near to her right hand. A bevy of judges, as aloof as herself from party politics, sits facing her. The wives of her Lords have been invited with their husbands, and sit among them on the crimson benches. And as if to emphasize that today's party is more a social than a political occasion, the members of the House of Commons, including most of the Ministers who conduct the business of state, stand humbly at the far end of the chamber, in the least conspicuous position of all. Here at the Bar is the reality of power; but today something is present which is more important than power, to which the wielders of power must do reverence.

Is all this symbolic ritual an anachronism, a meaningless mummery? Not unless all symbolism is delusion, not unless the monarchy itself is a mummery. To some, chiefly those minds obsessed with the limitless significance of politics, this is how it seems; and if the monarchy were a political institution they might be right. To others, with ears more sensitive to the pulse of a nation's heart, the great ceremonial of the royal opening of parliament is a parable of the subtle relationship of life to that limited aspect of life with which government is concerned, of human society to that department of society which we call the state. It is a timeless parable, as true today as in that dawn of history where stands the sacrificial king.

The sacrificial king is so universal a figure in the prehistory of nearly every people that he cannot be ignored without risk of distortion to our understanding of human nature itself. He has in him something of the magician, something of the priest, something of the mascot, perhaps something of the god – but, in his origins, if the informed conjectures of anthropology can be trusted, nothing at all of the ruler. He is the incarnate spirit of the tribe. He can be variously identified with the totem of the beasts they hunt, or with the products of the fields they till. With his life is mystically bound up the fertility of the herds and of the harvests, and the virility of the people themselves. So long as he is healthy and vigorous, the earth will yield its increase; his sickness may induce murrain and mildew, his death might entail general famine or starvation were it not possible to forestall it by replacing him – even ritually slaying him in many cases – with a younger successor. 'In the king's righteousness is the common weal, victory in war, mildness of the seasons, abundance of crops, freedom from pestilence. It is for the king to atone with God for the whole people.' The writer is not some primitive Teutonic medicine man in the depth of the primaeval forest. He is Alcuin of York, Abbot of St Martin's, Tours, the greatest Christian scholar of the Dark Ages and the intellectual fountainhead of the Carolingian Renaissance. The adhesion of this sophisticated mind to the immemorial tradition of sacrificial kingship shows that, though it may have been in the most remote past a concept of savagery and paganism, the central idea, of the mysterious inter-communion between a people and a dedicated man, is in itself neither pagan nor Christian, but derives from the deepest uncon-scious impulses of the human heart.

Christianity and all other forces of civilization have worked upon this conception through many centuries, overlaying the royal figure with new functions and powers (and later taking them away again), but without ever making obsolete the essential notion of the king as the supreme representative. Because he embodied the life of the people in an age when it was constantly in danger from external enemies, it was natural to choose for the office a man of known physical prowess capable of defending it; and so he very early became a leader in war. But, quoting Jolliffe again, 'to turn from the king as representative to the theory and practice of government, is to find him a vastly shrunken figure . . . We cannot say that there were no powers of kingship, but they were few, and thrust upon him by necessity.' Because his person was sacred, he had his 'peace' – meaning that acts of violence committed close to his dwelling-place were essentially sacrilegious, and could not be wholly atoned for by payment of compensation to the victim or his kin. Here is the beginning of criminal law; for breach of the king's peace, when that had been gradually extended from the palace precincts to the whole extent of the realm, would be seen as an offence against what would some day be called the state. Law was seen as the immemorial custom of the ancestors, which no living man could change; but the king came to be invoked as the arbitrator in disputes. With Ine and Alfred he became the collector and expositor of the customary laws. In the feudal age he acquired the character of the universal landlord, and the source of title to property; the president, also, of the council of lesser landlords, out of which would come parliament and at last, by slow and hesitant stages, the recognition of the possibility of making new law. In the fifteenth and sixteenth centuries all other authorities were successively subordinated and made derivative from the crown – the last to surrender being the church. So with the later Tudors the renaissance prince stands up in the plenitude of dominion, supreme over all interests spiritual or temporal, master not only of his subjects' bodies but also of their souls.

This was the conception of monarchy that the Tudors bequeathed to the Stuarts; but already the reaction was beginning. The sheet-anchor of individual liberty in the Middle Ages had been the division and balance of powers between temporal and spiritual authority, so that neither could command the whole man. With that anchor cut away, it was inevitable that the passion for freedom, innate in the English race, should seek fresh political outlets. So begins, at first in the turmoil of rebellion and civil war, the long process of breaking up the excessive concentration of power in the hands of the king. An experiment, transferring the whole of it to what became a military despotism, collapsed into anarchy with the death of the original despot; and the hereditary monarch was recalled to resume his place, though with impaired authority. The Whigs, hoping to seize the plenitude of power for the greater landed interest, drove out the ancient dynasty and substituted a foreign-born puppet; but in the fourth generation the puppet began to show that the royal institution still held a residue of strength undreamed of in the Whig philosophy. Then in the nineteenth and twentieth centuries a continuous movement, led for most of the time by the Liberals, gradually redistributed the whole of the strictly political powers of the wearer of the crown to wider and wider classes, culminating in manhood and womanhood suffrage within recent memory. The last effective power of the monarchy to intervene in politics appears to have become atrophied within the present decade. It was the right of the Sovereign, on the occurrence of a vacancy in the office of prime minister, to choose from among the leaders of the party in power that one who in her personal judgement was best qualified, in the interest not of the party but of the whole nation, to hold the highest place. The claim to transfer this right of choice to the party machine, originally made by the Labour party but since slavishly followed by the Conservatives, was surely unconstituional at its inception; but, like many another innovation in a system governed by precedent, must no doubt now be regarded as legitimated in retrospect.

With the practical obsolescence of this last personal function in politics, Elizabeth II stands now entirely denuded of all authority over the process of government. Her personal influence is quite another matter; it may be very great, and, as Bagehot observed, increases every year by reason of the continuous growth of her personal experience of the business of state, while parties and ministers come and go. But speaking in terms of command as distinct from persuasion, the whole of the powers possessed by the Tudor sovereigns has been successively relinquished, most of them to the prime minister and Cabinet, who during the tenure of office between elections today wield more arbitrary authority than was in practice exerted by the most absolute of our sixteenth-century monarchs. (I have indeed argued elsewhere[1] that there remains one dormant power, the power to dismiss the government and dissolve parliament, which could be used once and once only to frustrate a totalitarian conspiracy against the liberties of the people, on the condition of staking the existence of the monarchy itself upon the outcome of an appeal to the electorate). It remains true that all this alienation of personal authority has in no way diminished the true strength of the monarchy; that Elizabeth II, deprived of all power to control the actions of her ministers or her parliament, retains a surer hold upon the allegiance and devotion of her subjects than was possessed by Elizabeth I at the height of her despotic power.

What has become steadily more apparent in the constitutional development since the accession of Queen Victoria is that every

---

[1] *The Work of the Queen*, 1958, pp. 165-67.

stage of withdrawal from direct participation in government has been a stage of closer identification with the life of the people. As the accretions of the centuries upon the central substance have dropped away from the monarchy, the rock upon which it is founded has stood out more conspicuously. By the surrender of political authority it has been in no degree weakened: on the contrary, it has refreshed itself from the original fount of its life. The crown has been converted into a metaphor for the executive arm of government, which is wielded by the leaders of party. The Queen remains, in undiminished splendour, as the supreme representative, which none of her predecessors has ever ceased to be, since the days of the mystical-magical king of prehistory.

Though the mystique and the magic have been transformed and transformed again through the ages in response to changing ways of thought about God, man and nature, the Queen still fulfils the need that called that remote figure into being. It is necessary for every human community sometimes to feel as one, to think as one, to possess some institution that can express the shared emotion by symbolic words or action. Of that necessity monarchy was born, and continues. (It is etymologically unfortunate that the word we cannot avoid using contains the element $\dot{\alpha}\rho\chi\dot{\eta}$, rule, which is not part of the original concept of kingship.) Monarchy is the natural form of human society: of society, which is something other than the state. Monarchy is much older than the state; it is older even than the church, under whose protection the state as we know it in England grew up. Many modern nations have lost their monarchies, generally as a result of foreign conquest or internal revolution during the period when the adventitious political element in kingship had been allowed to predominate. These now have to meet the psychological need with inferior substitutes, such as a constitution or a flag – inferior because artificial, and therefore superficial, with no natural hold upon the human heart, so that they have to be laboriously commended by politicians, teachers or propagandists. England, having been for many centuries exempt from foreign invasion, and having speedily recovered long ago from its republican revolution, has been able to preserve its monarchy as the supreme representative symbol, and allegiance thereto as its natural way of life.

The Queen is accepted as the indisputable representative of

her people, and therefore the guarantor of their unity, because she is the head of society not only in its generalized sense, but separately of each of its aspects or departments. She is the source of justice, which is impartially measured out to the people by judges acting in her name. Her symbolic patronage dignifies the work of science through the Royal Society, or the arts through the Royal Academy; royal appointments and foundations in the universities preserve the recognition that the life of learning is a service to the people, for whom she speaks. She is the fountain of honour, so that the accolades or the medals that she distributes come to their recipients as expressions of the gratitude of the whole nation. Because the armed services wear her uniform and their officers hold her commission, it is visibly shown that they exist to defend the entire body of the people, incarnate in their representative, and not to advance the interest of any section or party in the state.

But more important than any of these functions, which could be discharged, though less well, by an elected president or some constitutional abstraction, is the representation of the people in their private and domestic life. She herself must live a great deal of her private life in public. Thereby she holds up a mirror in which her subjects may feel that they see an image of themselves at their best, of their life as they would wish it to be if they could all breathe the spacious air (as they imagine it) of palaces. It is a magnifying but not, it is to be hoped, a distorting mirror. It feeds their pride in their national glory; but because the person it reflects is not a superhuman genius, but an ordinary woman like themselves, it is the real national virtues that are glorified. It is for her to give them a sense of the capacity of the ordinary man or woman in the extraordinary place, and therefore of the latent capacity of themselves in the ordinary places they occupy. Sometimes they see her as a figure robed and crowned, in dazzling splendour as a symbol of all that the nation has achieved in history; sometimes she moves familiarly among them, taking always the centre to the circumference, and speaking to the humble of their everyday concerns. The power to see the two aspects in proportion, to fuse in the mind the two conceptions of the hieratic symbol and the familiar friend, is the art of living in a monarchy.

It is essential to this conception of royalty that the sovereign should be seen against the background of consort and family, should hold up a pattern of domestic life in which the people can see their own domestic virtues idealized. (It was because Edward VIII contemplated a kind of domesticity, legitimate enough for lesser persons by the permitted standards of the age, but such as the great central body of public opinion could not idealize, that the national instinct rejected him.) The insatiable public interest in the most trifling details of Royal Family life emphasizes what on other grounds is seen to be true, that a social or representative monarchy necessarily requires hereditary succession. The prevailing fashion of the day repudiates the hereditary principle as a title to political authority. There has been no corresponding rejection of heredity as the cement of social cohesion. The ordinary man still expects and wishes to be succeeded, in his place in society as in his material possessions, by his own children and not by strangers selected by vote or by computer as the persons most rationally qualified to wear his shoes and carry on where he left off. It follows that, if the monarchy is truly to represent the common man, its continuity must be secured by the same natural process. Thus also is it enabled to stand symbolically for the unity of the nation throughout its existence in time. The people give their allegiance to themselves symbolized and personified in an unbroken line of human beings stretching backward, and also forward, through the ages, in whose name their ancestors won the fame of England, in whose honour their descendants will lay the laurels of the future at the foot of the ancient throne.

The representative sovereign, as has been said, is the head of society both as a whole and in each of its several aspects. One of these aspects is the state, which is society organized for politics. Thus to express the relation is to assert the subordination of politics to the whole of life, a subordination of which the person of the social monarch is the guarantor. As head of society, and also head of the state within society, the Queen's place in politics has the subtlety characteristic of ancient things. The personal powers, even as possessed by Queen Victoria, have dwindled to practically nothing. The influence upon government remains very little changed since Bagehot, more than a century ago, analysed it as the right to be informed, the right to encourage and the right to warn. It may be far-reaching, and may increase continually with the growth of the sovereign's experience. But fundamentally the office of the monarch is not now to wield power, but to keep power in its subordinate place. It is an English characteristic to regard the worship of power as vulgar. No sort of mystique is allowed to transfigure the prosaic figures of our actual rulers. As a law-abiding people we give our obedience to the ministers of the crown; but we give our reverence to the Queen.

Her presence at the head of society sets a limit to ambition. Whether such a limit is to be desired is of course open to debate. Every American child is taught that in his country there is no limit: that there is no law to prevent him – or even her – from ending up as president. The English have always distrusted that philosophy, perhaps from an instinctive fear that the man who by fending for himself has forced his way to the very top may go on fending for himself when he has arrived there. In our country we are glad that the summit is not open to competition. A politician raised to that eminence – or for that matter a military commander as has lately happened in many countries including the United States, France and Spain – can never become the focus of national unity in the same sense as a hereditary monarch. There is always a defeated candidate nursing resentment; there is always an opposition party hoping to turn the tables at the next election – or the next *coup d'état*. But under our more mature and fortunate system opposition is able *reculer pour mieux sauter* without endangering the cohesion of society; and a party in power is continually reminded of its duty to the whole community and not merely to the section to whose votes it owes its mandate to govern.

For it is by something more than a legal fiction that the mandate is not conveyed directly, but mediated through the Queen, who gives her commission where the majority have given their trust, but gives it in the name not of the majority but of the whole. It is by virtue of this quality of representation in the sovereign, in an age progressively less sensitive to the sacramental consecration of her person from which historically the representation derives, that the real possessors of power are continually reminded that they hold it in trust from one who is not herself powerful but is nevertheless more important than they. Prime ministers present their humble duty, expound their policies and plans, and listen respectfully to any criticisms the Queen may be graciously pleased to offer. Commanders-in-chief stand to attention and salute. In the highest appellate tribunal of the Commonwealth the judges, having reached final unanimity on the weightiest problems of the law, 'humbly advise Her Majesty accordingly'. All alike in their most solemn actions and in the exercise of their widest powers, profess themselves to be servants, formally of the Queen, but by implication servants of the people, unified and incarnate in her. These forms of humility enjoined upon the great have their psychological effect throughout the body politic. They are a constant warning to our effective rulers against the illusion that the source of their authority is in themselves. Therein, perhaps more than in any constitutional safeguards that exist or could be devised, resides the chief security of our liberties against dictatorship.

In the world of the twentieth century the British monarchy is unique. After the hurricane of the French Revolution and the Napoleonic wars, when, in Elizabeth Browning's phrase, 'kings crept out again to feel the sun', they were all restored to their thrones on quasi-contractual terms; so that those of their heirs who survive in Europe today are imprisoned in the forms of nineteenth-century constitutions. They are officials, hereditary no doubt, but with functions defined for them in a dated document. By contrast, the royalty of Windsor preserves the timeless essence of monarchy itself; it is free to change and develop its functions in correspondence with the changing aspects of the people it represents. It has in fact been continuously changing throughout history; yet *plus ça change plus c'est la même chose*, and, by contrast with a rigidly limited eighteenth-century institution like the American presidency, it is always up to date.

And, having changed and changed again through so many centuries (in its accidents, as a scholastic philosopher would say, not its substance), it is certain that the monarchy will go on changing through the centuries to come. One function which has been deliberately omitted from the foregoing pages seems – regrettably – not unlikely to fall away. Just as the sovereign represents the unity of the nation in time, so he has until recently represented the unity of the Empire (a larger and more liberating word than Commonwealth) in space. So long as the same person was separately accepted as the head of society in each of its linked nations, their union, in a sense transcending politics, could be felt as a living reality. The abandonment of the monarchical forms by so many is a tacit recognition that the Empire has failed to draw into an organic whole those of its members who are heirs of non-British civilizations, or have no indigenous civilizations at all. There remain (if the probable secession of Ceylon may be anticipated) only Gibraltar, a few islands, and the three oversea realms of predominantly European settlement; and signs are not wanting that even in these the strain of maintaining the sense of social representation by a personage so rarely seen, against the centrifugal trend of political nationalism, may be beyond the strength of the Queen's successors. It is safest to think of the future of the monarchy in the context only of the British Isles.

Some pessimists even here fear that the monarchy may be undermined by the destruction of some of its supporting institutions. The last speech from the throne put by ministers into the Queen's mouth announced the intention of the professional politicians, who have reduced the Lower House to subjection, to seize control of the Upper as well. If the hereditary peers, the last representatives in politics of the amateur spirit which has served English history so honourably, are driven out of the House of Lords and it is wholly abandoned to the caucus nominees, the monarchy will be left isolated, say these pessimists, as the only example of a hereditary institution in the community. Thus isolated, can it survive? A twofold answer may be tendered. First, the statement that the monarchy will be the only remaining hereditary institution is not true: the private family, the toughest and most fundamental institution, is likely to remain essentially hereditary for a good many generations yet, and it is this that the social monarchy especially reflects and represents. Secondly, the extrusion of the peers of long descent from their place in government, lamentable though the prospect is, would be in itself a process merely political, and is not directly relevant to the place of the monarchy outside and above politics. It is a matter of conjecture whether the social prestige of ancient lineage can survive the rebellion against the hereditary function in government; provided that it does, such support as the social monarchy derives from its presence need not be seriously affected.

Finally, the one function that the monarchy can never abdicate without ceasing to exist is that of representation. The people are sovereign, but the Sovereign is the people; they are one and indivisible. For that reason, to predict the future of the monarchy is to foretell the whole development of generations yet unborn: an impossible undertaking. The monarchy will surely remain, as it has always been, infinitely adaptable. Even in politics, as Mr Geoffrey Dennis has somewhere written, it could adjust itself if necessary to a communist revolution: we should be governed by Her Majesty's Soviets. The rising generation will no doubt impose its own new interpretation on the monarchy, as every generation before it has done. But there is little sign that the young are turning away from the throne: at present they seem much more inclined to turn away from the politicians. As these last words are written, the *Daily Mail* publishes the result of an opinion poll, taken to determine which personalities in the contemporary world are most popular with British adolescents. The majority vote gives first place to 'Mother'; but the second to the Queen.

JEREMY MURRAY-BROWN

Jeremy Murray-Brown was born in 1932 in the North-West Frontier Province of India. He was educated at Winchester College and New College, Oxford, where he took a first class honours degree in Modern History. His National Service was with the KRRC. In 1955 he joined the BBC television service where he worked in the current affairs department. As a producer of 'Panorama' he travelled widely, including visits to Moscow, the Far East, Africa and America. In 1962 he left the BBC and has since worked as a freelance television producer-director. In this capacity he produced a special edition of 'Panorama' in November 1966 on the occasion of Prince Charles's eighteenth birthday. He is married and has three children.

LIFTING THE CURTAIN

JEREMY MURRAY-BROWN

Whenever he heard the National Anthem played on the radio my grandfather used to stand up. He was a much loved and respected figure and my brother and I had to follow suit. He looked after us during the war, while my parents were in India, and his influence was strong and lasting. I cannot now think of the monarchy without recalling those scenes from my childhood.

Nor can I think of the war itself without remembering the impression made on us by the King. Through him we became aware of how serious the Battle of Britain really was, which otherwise struck boys like us as exciting and even as fun. What went to the heart of our experience was the voice of the King broadcasting after the nine o'clock news. Winston Churchill, of course, gripped our imagination in a different way; he was the hero figure whom we recognized from our nursery histories. The King's message was simpler, more direct and personal. We suffered with him over his stammer, we understood what he was trying to say, and we stood up when the National Anthem was played at the end.

As a result of his wartime impact on us, I suppose, I later found George VI's funeral a most moving occasion. I was undergoing my national service and was positioned with a detachment of my regiment at Hyde Park Corner. As the cortège passed slowly by, greeted all along the route by the sad command of 'reverse arms', each member of the crowd seemed to withdraw into himself. I could sense this with my fellow recruits who came mostly from the East End of London. For everyone who watched the melancholy pageantry set off a private stream of associations. Mine began with those broadcasts and scenes of the Royal Family in the Blitz and passed through adolescent dreams about princesses to 'ad portas' in my time at Winchester and the picture of that last agonizing farewell to his daughter at the airport.

Each generation must have this nostalgic affection for the monarchy, and feel the emotional tie of its own childhood impressions. A generation before mine saw King George V's jubilee, the last great pageant of Empire. A generation before that endured the horrors of the First World War fighting for King against Kaiser. How many families cherish on their walls a framed inscription signed by the King which touched them by its courtly message: 'He whom this scroll commemorates was numbered among those who at the call of king and country left all that was dear to them ... that others might live in freedom. I join with my grateful people in sending you this memorial of a brave life given for others in the Great War. George R. I.' A generation after mine had as the focus of their emotional attachment the memory of the coronation of Queen Elizabeth; and a generation after that, perhaps, the tragic pictures of the Queen at Aberfan.

In 1966, while preparing a television documentary about the monarchy, I came to look closer at some of the trappings of the system. It was a curious experience and with its sudden, comic, revelations almost as moving as that funeral had been. Like a scene shift in a play it introduced to me new props and characters and released a different set of images.

The most notable of these is the brougham which, as it clatters down The Mall, like the entry of the porter in Macbeth, interrupts the sense of high drama to which one face of monarchy constantly plays. Every weekday morning at ten o'clock, gleaming and smelling of warm leather, the brougham pulls up at the Privy Purse entrance to Buckingham Palace. The Queen's messenger loads it with her 'boxes', the red and blue leather cases containing state papers, calls out the order of the ministries for which they are destined, and away it rattles to Whitehall, St James's or Petty France. In the traffic jams of Mayfair and Piccadilly this strange vehicle can often be seen competing with buses and taxis, its finely liveried coachman and the sleek horse both casting the same disdainful glance at the hubbub around them.

Is the brougham part of twentieth-century monarchy? Do state papers have to travel by coach and horse? No foreigner would believe it, no secret agent credit that blueprints and plans, Foreign Office telegrams and cabinet memoranda, might pass in so quaint a manner between the Queen and her ministers. Yet how beguiling is the arrangement; for if the sovereign must read all these documents – and we are assured that this is part of the essential function of monarchy – what more appropriate device could be chosen to symbolize that obscure constitutional rôle? The brougham belongs to the same charade as the Duke of Norfolk, Black Rod and Garter King-of-Arms. To give them a modern 'image', say a minivan instead of the brougham, or a serving general instead of the Earl Marshal, would raise questions about their real significance. Who would cheer for a king on a scooter?

This face of monarchy is like a waxworks happening. The crowds come to the forecourt of Buckingham Palace as they might to Madame Tussaud's and they watch the Changing of the Guard in the same spirit as they would the dumb show in the Hall of Kings. At Madame Tussaud's itself visitors may be observed suddenly to lower their voices as they enter the Great Hall and approach the royal tableau. In a pool of bright light and colour, dummies of the Queen and Prince Philip, surrounded by those of relatives and other royal figures, draw hushed and respectful attention while, nearby, models of glum prime ministers are lucky to receive a glance. Monarchs know the value of such folk myths. As the canons of Westminster Abbey, alarmed at the crowds' deserting their shrines for St Paul's when Nelson was buried there, commissioned their own effigy of the great admiral, so the Palace has for long co-operated with Tussauds in arranging sittings to keep their wax doubles' appearances up to date.

Here then is the paradox of our monarchy. On the one hand is its undoubted emotional appeal which is capable still of bringing a tear to the eye. On the other hand are its archaic rituals, its symbolism and its essential tattiness. Most people like the monarchy and respect the Queen, but how much, they wonder, is it worth? How far does it preserve an outmoded social system? 'Mystique by Moss Bros', as the credits might read. The further one goes down the corridors of the Palace, one feels, the more threadbare the carpets must become. When the time comes, how shall I explain that brougham to *my* grandchildren?

In one form or another present-day discussions about the monarchy revolve around this paradox. It is the theme which links the essays in this book. They do not claim to be an exact cross-section of opinion on the subject, but a collection of individual views. The lesson of the polls is that few people defend the out and out 'magic of monarchy' approach any longer and as few are out and out republicans. Most people want to see the paradox resolved. But those who might give a lead in this, the intelligentsia, are largely bored with the subject. The danger is that the monarchy's own built-in inertia may not be able to overcome the country's apathy and indifference.

Open debate of the kind expressed by the varied contributions to this book is itself a healthy sign for the future. It is welcome to find authors who feel the subject is important enough to be worth an essay. The publication of a book like this, like the production of a special 'Panorama' report on the monarchy, shows how revolutionary has been the change in the climate in which communications media now work compared with ten years ago. At that time the Press and Broadcasting Establishment ganged up against Malcolm Muggeridge with vicious hostility for saying far less than is now permitted on, say, late night satirical shows on television. It is encouraging that the cartoonists who are represented here have been able to break the taboos which existed on such drawings for over half a century; but few periodicals would have published them ten years ago.

Monarchy cannot operate in a vacuum from which all such critical air has been expelled since it is the oxygen which Prince Charles's generation breathes. The dilemma is that monarchy's main contribution to the twentieth century, so it seems to those who run it, is to delay changes and not promote them; to act as an emollient not as a catalyst; to sooth the bruised pride of Empire with the balm of the Commonwealth idea. No one has put this better than Harold Nicolson in his classic biography of George V: 'In an epoch of change, he remains the symbol of continuity; in a phase of disintegration, the element of cohesion; in times of mutability, the emblem of permanence ... The appeal of hereditary monarchy is to stability rather than change, to continuity rather than to experiment, to custom rather than to novelty, to safety rather than to adventure.'

These are the principles which guide the men and women who assist the Queen in her work. They are the Palace officials, the Royal Household of 'advisers' whose hands can be seen dimly in the background of the 'boxes', whose figures move discreetly beside the Queen whenever she performs an official duty in public, whose eyes screen all that passes between Buckingham Palace and the public. Theirs is a role which has no constitutional basis. Harold Laski defined the sovereign's Private Secretary as half statesman, half lackey, able 'to deflect the lightning from others' and 'to carry the burden of the sovereign's mistakes'. In the past men who could meet these qualifications came largely from the armed services, forming almost a caste of their own. Recent recruits, however, have been drawn from the Civil Service and the future may well see a tendency for the Palace secretariat to transform itself into something approaching a government department. Though no one questions their high standards of integrity this is scarcely a move which will produce the changes most people want.

In a sense, however, the move would be logical as it would cement more firmly the link between Number 10 Downing Street and Buckingham Palace. For the real target for criticism of the way our monarchy works is those other 'advisers', the Queen's ministers. It is they who, according to constitutional theory, must accept formal responsibility for all that the Queen says or does; whether they like it or not, it is they who operate a constitutional monarchy.

These are the men who choose to maintain the fictions symbolized by the brougham and who ultimately seek to benefit from the folk myths of Madame Tussaud's. One public opinion poll has stated that almost a third of the population believes the Queen is someone special chosen by God. Our special television enquiry showed that no less than 70 per cent of the population believes that the Queen, in some form or other, exercises power to affect important decisions. The paradox makes sense only when it is seen that politicians alone draw comfort from concealing realities about the monarchy beneath these popular misconceptions.

The truth is that nothing now remains of the powers and prerogatives which were once thought to belong to the sovereign. The reforms of Sir Alec Douglas Home in the method by which Conservatives elect their leader, and the Labour Party's declaration in January 1957, have made it clear that constitutional orthodoxy now requires the Crown to wait for the political parties to take the initiative in deciding who should be the nation's prime minister. As for the formal act of dissolving parliament, the only kind of emergency in which the sovereign might wield this power independently of the government of the day would involve a constitutional punch-up from which few of our democratic institutions would emerge unscathed. The crown's role in parliament is but a more gorgeous version of Madame Tussaud's wax model; it would be as unlikely for the one to speak out of turn as for the other to blink.

Yet many people still believe that the Queen does intervene in the administration of the country. Phrases such as 'royal pardon' lend credibility to the popular misconception that the sovereign is personally the fountain of mercy. But as George VI discovered, when he was unable to obtain from Herbert Morrison reprieves for two murderers sentenced to death, the prerogative of mercy works only on the recommendation of the Home Secretary and not on the sovereign's initiative. The kind of influence exerted on a prime minister by the sovereign at their private meetings is impossible to gauge. The personal relationship between them is said to be valuable and may be decisive in small matters, but it is more likely that prime ministers exploit it for internal political purposes.

The crown was for long thought of as the fount of honour and investitures at Buckingham Palace shed the mystical glamour of tradition indiscriminately on those who served their fellow men, their political parties and their king. But the Beatles' MBE's signalled the end of the losing battle which sovereigns had waged over honours for many years. George V once plaintively remarked after his request for a knighthood to be given an inventor had been turned down flat: 'As I so seldom ask for a knighthood I really think that I might be treated with anyhow some consideration occasionally.' Supposedly, awards to the Victorian Order remain at the sovereign's sole discretion. But can anyone seriously believe that the Queen would have been allowed to grant Sir Humphrey Gibbs the KCVO if this had contradicted the British government's Rhodesia policy? Politicians find it easy to exploit public confusion over the origination and direction of royal patronage.

In these and other ways the doctrine of constitutional advice, which requires that every public word and deed of the sovereign must be endorsed by the government, has been turned inside out. Instead of its reserve powers being regarded as a check on the executive the monarchy is called on to lend the executive extra-parliamentary authority. At a Lord Mayor's banquet Harold Wilson put the deception most openly when he said: 'I do not need to tell an audience such as this at the heart of the Common-wealth that any instructions or command issued by Her Majesty's ministers in the name of the Queen could not and would not in any circumstances be issued without the specific authority and approval of Her Majesty herself.'

So in the double-talk of constitutional propriety the brougham image of monarchy is manipulated by the politicians. Outwardly harmless as it trundles around the West End, it seems no more than a pleasant piece of show for the tourists and a meaningless curiosity to passers-by. But for the politicians what it symbolizes remains a possible cover for unpopular or unscrupulous acts, such as Orders in Council invoking executive powers which have been left deliberately unspecific in legislation.

So long as voters believe that the monarch influences policies, ministers will fly to Balmoral to take part in the ancient ritual of a Privy Council meeting. Thus the legal fiction of the sovereign's participation in government can be used to bypass parliament while the politicians hide behind the throne. The ghosts of the Star Chamber must smile at this modern resort to the crown's authority 'in the national interest'.

There is a story that when the post-war Labour government was examining the Palace for possible economies in the running of the monarchy, court officials suggested that the most obvious sacrifice would be the Royal Mews. 'Would that mean giving up the coaches?' the politicians asked, and on being told that this was so, they at once rejected the idea. So the brougham and all that it signifies survived. But so too for the Palace did the austere regime. The Queen's Civil List had built into it a 'supplemen-tary provision' against inflation; but it was apportioned in 1952 by a Conservative government which was elected with a small majority in the House and an overall minority in the country. Tories did not wish to seem to give too much to the new sovereign. So the monarchy's finances were set at a level which has proved inadequate for some years. But the demands of the state have increased: greater numbers of visiting dignitaries, whom the Foreign Office wishes to impress, are wheeled into Buckingham Palace for lunch or dinner; more and more diplomats requiring the same round of etiquette must be entertained by the Queen; the sham conventions of the Commonwealth have to be honoured by Royal Tours. All these rising expenses fall on the devalued

Civil List causing it to run at an annual loss which has been estimated at being about 30 per cent of the total. The Queen makes up this deficiency out of her private fortune. Too proud to confront her ministers with the situation, she risks impoverishing herself to meet their requirements.

Here the politicians are at their most unscrupulous. We must have a head of state, and the value we place on the ceremonial which necessarily accompanies his or her functions is a measure of the value we place on the state itself. Why not, then, submit the Civil List to annual parliamentary approval like every other financial measure of the government? Rather than face open debate on the cost of the monarchy, and accept its worth realistically, the politicians prefer to leave uncorrected the idea, which many people have, that royalty is a waste and an extravagance. Governments which have succeeded in bankrupting the nation would not flinch from bankrupting the Queen.

If we are to think of the monarchy as no more than a parliamentary convenience, there seems no future for it but fossilization in the doctrinal clay of 'advice'. But the truth is that the country is moving away from its old parliamentary base, politicians have become discredited, and governments give the impression of no longer being fully in control of the nation's affairs. Other power structures within the state have grown up since Bagehot's day and each of these is more or less independent of parliamentary control – the trade unions, the communications media, giant industrial corporations, state-owned commercial enterprises, an emancipated university population. At the political level regional loyalties have directly challenged the central legislature, and the old ideological appeal of 'Westminster-style democracy' makes little impact in a post-imperialist era. These currents offer new and wider opportunities for the monarchy. Without discarding its constitutional anchor the royal galleon can afford to ride closer to the people and engage in a more personal dialogue with them.

Take for example the Christmas broadcasts. They are the only occasion in the year when the head of state speaks to the people in the people's medium. But a Christmas broadcast is not a dialogue at all; it is a monologue delivered with charm and grace which quite fails to communicate, it is a broadcasting equivalent of a speech from the throne.

Yet when the Christmas broadcasts were inaugurated by George V in 1932 they proved to be a tremendous success. Many writers trace the rise of modern 'popular' monarchy to this factor. When the king broadcast on the evening of his silver jubilee his voice almost broke with emotion, so overwhelming had been his welcome during the day from the crowds in London's poor quarters. 'I'd no idea they felt like this about me,' he said afterwards, 'I am beginning to think they must really like me for myself.' By using the radio the king had, for the first time, been able to reach out to all the people universally and indiscriminately. He had, quite literally, spoken over the heads of the politicians and the courtiers and all the hangers-on to royalty, so that it seemed to every listener at home that there was no constitutional barrier between him and the monarch.

Furthermore he coughed slightly in the middle of his sentence. So the king was real after all, listeners felt. A wax dummy would not cough. Harold Nicholson described the effect.

'The King, an unreal incredible personage, a resplendent hierophant bowing rhythmically in a golden coach, with diamond orb and sceptre in his hands, suddenly became a human voice – intimate and paternal – speaking to them in their own living rooms, speaking to them from a box on the table between the sewing-machine and the mug. "I am speaking," the voice continued, "to the children above all. Remember children, the King is speaking to *you*." His was a wonderful voice – strong, emphatic, vibrant, with undertones of sentiment, devoid of all condescension, artifice or pose. The effect was wide and deep.'

'Surely there was magic in all this,' he added. Others thought so too, and the Christmas broadcast became part of the formula for a successful monarchy, its impact still felt by boys during the last war.

Now the magic has worn off. In 1958 the Queen delivered the Christmas message for the first time on television, but this new 'marvel of science' failed to do for her what radio had done for her grandfather. The reason was not just the technical disadvantage from which a woman suffers on television, but because the image presented was by then no more than an 'image'. Thirty years before a disembodied voice on the air left the imagination free, but in the 1960s a figure directly facing the camera and speaking into the lens is marked as an advertiser, or politician, or lecturer. It is not a human and intimate style and it only succeeds if it is practised frequently enough to become part of television's own folk-lore. Used for a royal broadcast it emphasizes how out of date the formula has become.

For a time this failure did not matter. The Queen brought to the throne greater mystical allure than any of her predecessors, and she had no need to seek popularity through television, or indeed through any other medium. The job was done for her by others, and by no one so effectively, or so devotedly, as Richard Dimbleby.

His death has deprived the monarchy of its television champion. No one could replace him in the role. So the future offers the Queen an opportunity for breaking out of the cage of formality in which the old broadcasting formula has restricted her. She could turn her television appearances into more intimate and conversational occasions; she could permit interviews; on carefully selected occasions she could act as hostess to the nation and introduce special programmes. She could lift the restrictions on microphones which are at present set on film and television cameras, so that all they are allowed to record are the formal, processed, utterances and not the human touches. (Few, as a result, now bother to cover routine royal events.) In short, she could deploy the arts of communication in an up to date manner, as Prince Philip has done, and as Prince Charles shows signs of being able to do, and engage in a genuine dialogue with the people.

No doubt there are advisers who fear the constitutional implications of the sovereign's becoming involved in topical controversies on television. Prince Philip, they might say, is in a different position. The Queen does not allow him to see state papers and he is not bound by the doctrine of constitutional advice. The same argument, however, might apply to the Prince of Wales and it is unlikely that he will remain publicly dumb throughout the years in which he is heir to the throne. The Queen owes it to the future to brave these difficulties. We are surely an intelligent enough people now to be able to distinguish between moral and political issues; and if the politicians were to fear that the sovereign might embarrass them, the BBC could always introduce a royal broadcast with a disclaimer: 'What follows are

Her Majesty's own thoughts and words; they do not necessarily represent official government policy.'

That kind of royal broadcast may be a long way off; another way in which the monarchy could engage in a closer dialogue with people is, in the most literal sense, simply by talking to them. This may seem an unfair comment when one considers the arduous programme of public duties which the Queen undertakes each year. By her stamina and technical skill in handling these she inspires admiration from her staff and respect from all those she meets.

But are they the right people she meets? Why invite a film star to lunch rather than a film technician, or a trade union official than a man from the shop floor? And what happens when the Queen does tour the provinces?

A few months ago I had an opportunity to follow a typical royal procession through towns on the south-east coast. The Queen's day began at Battle where she was met by the Duke of Norfolk, Lord Lieutenant of the County, his face a Tudor portrait and his bearing something from the first Elizabethan age; and it ended with a tea party for civic dignitaries in Eastbourne's town hall. Between lay an unremitting series of handshakes, addresses, visits and presentations, the last taking place literally at the swing doors of the town hall as the royal party were leaving. A bewildering succession of Sussex folk bowed and curtsied to her – mayors and mayoresses, aldermen, sheriffs, chief constables, schoolmasters, schoolmistresses, clerks to the local councils, magistrates, deans, vicars, vicars' wardens, managers of building works, hotel-keepers who could not very well be avoided as they were providing the lunch, college students and school prefects, the odd Lord and Lady who also could not very easily be excluded, and a man officially described as 'a representative fisherman' who presented the Queen with a basketful of Rye bloaters. Prince Philip was made a member of a winkle club, and the Queen also collected an electronic game of noughts and crosses for the royal children ('and we feel in our hearts that the not-so-young royal children will also play with this game'). Together they signed countless books. In amongst it all, the Queen had time to pay a private call on a horse she had once owned which was now stabled with the Mayor of Rye. The crowds along the route cheered, which pleased the Lord Lieutenant: 'I was proud of my Sussex people today.' Children were allowed the day off school and waved Union Jacks, press and television reporters scurried from spot to appointed spot, leap-frogging the itinerary in order to keep up with it.

This was the mystique of monarchy in action without a doubt. They all saw her for a fleeting moment. They caught the colour of her clothes, perhaps, or overheard some formal greeting before the detectives blocked out the view and the procession moved on. 'I blinked,' said one schoolboy, 'and missed her going past.' 'Was it worth it?' 'Well, she means more to me than Harold Wilson does anyway!'

Yet there was left among the crowd the feeling that it had all been too rushed, and that the Queen had met too limited a selection of people. All those chosen were pillars of the community, no doubt, even the fisherman with his bloaters, but there had been no real communication with the people who had turned out to cheer. One scene stands out in my mind. As the party drew up for lunch at a hotel in Hastings, a line of Old Contemptibles positioned immediately beside the entrance came smartly to attention while the Queen walked in. It would have taken her a few minutes only to have paused and spoken to one of the veterans, and the gesture would have meant more to everyone else who had waited there than all the other formal presentations. But her officials had briefed her to keep to the timetable ('and she's such a small person she can't really mix with crowds'), so the old soldiers had to be ignored.

These tours are a hard and costly grind for all who take part in them and they deserve to be exploited better, since the relationship between the monarchy and the regional forces at work in Britain today could be important. Better communication between Crown and people would help offset the impersonality of modern governments and fill the vacuum left by the disintegration of our parliamentary system. But this means opting for a more spontaneous approach to these tours and relying less on the official screening which goes on beforehand. Greater allowance for unrehearsed exchanges with individuals in the crowd would enable the sovereign to cut through the barricade of local worthies, just as a different style of royal broadcast could reach out over the heads of the politicians at Westminster.

Giving the monarchy such a direction would not come easily

to those other 'advisers', the members of the royal household. With the collapse of the old establishment they have lost confidence in their ability to control the future. They are fearful of making any new move. One of them might put it like this: 'I feel as if we are sitting on the top of a glacier not knowing if at any moment it will begin to slide.' Changes, they all feel, will have incalculable consequences. Peering out beyond the ornate gates of Buckingham Palace, as the brougham sets off down The Mall, they see it assailed by a jumble of conflicting opinions, paradoxes and prejudices, but they entrust to its creaking springs their hopes and fears for the institution they serve, its only protection its utter unreality. They will not step outside themselves to test opinion nor encourage their sovereign to meet the public boldly as Richard II once braved Wat Tyler and the peasants.

Is there any need for such caution? A courtier would reply: 'I am a monarchist. To admit the need for public relations would be defeatist.' Such an attitude may be sincere and honourable, but it is scarcely contemporary, and shows no readiness to 'change with the times'. Nor is there any historical justification for it. In the past advice of a nature we should now describe as 'P.R.' was offered by courtiers without prompting and without shame. Writing to King George V after the republican outburst which briefly followed the fall of the Czars in 1917 Lord Stamfordham, the King's Private Secretary, counselled: 'We must endeavour to induce the thinking working classes, Socialist and others, to regard the crown, not as a figure-head, and as an institution which, as they put it, "don't count", but as a living power for good, with receptive faculties affecting the interests and social well-being of all classes, and ready, not only to sympathize with those questions but anxious to further their solution.' George V was sensitive to public opinion and forced his governments to react to it. It was in response to what he thought people wanted that he adopted the name of Windsor for his House to allay any suspicion that the monarchy was pro-German.

'A living power for good' – it is a worth while objective still for the monarchy to pursue. As the Queen grows older her example and experience could become powerful influences. One courtier described the next five years as a period in the doldrums for the monarchy. Yet this is the very opportunity for it to wield its influence as a moral force in the country, a role which governments reject. But to achieve this, for people to respect the monarchy for what it is and not for what suits the politicians, the style must change. And to promote changes with this objective is not a degrading use of P.R. principles.

At the beginning of King George V's reign, when parliament was elected by only a sixth of the population, the Crown could well consider itself holding prerogative powers in reserve 'in the national interest' on behalf of the disenfranchised. Monarchy, at that time, had genuine constitutional importance and was involved, as a result, in actual political controversies. Today that importance has gone, eroded by the growth of the two-party system based on full adult suffrage. But the decadence of our parliamentary system gives a new meaning to the phrase 'in the national interest'. More than ever it requires that the monarchy takes the initiative in standing out 'as a living power for good'. And it can only do this by direct communication between the sovereign and the people, not with archaic constitutional rituals.

Most people welcome and respect moral leadership, though it is often derided and provides good ammunition for the satirists. It is what is symbolized for me by my grandfather's reaction to the National Anthem. He recognized in the monarchy qualities of loyalty, incorruptibility and the readiness to serve others, and he set the same standards for himself. Changes in the formal style of monarchy would enhance and not diminish this appeal. Its influence works today by closer acquaintance and not by standing off, by actuality not reported speech. At the same time I should hope that changes need not eliminate the private eccentricities of our monarchy. Perhaps when the Queen does come to give a conducted tour of her palaces for world distribution by television, she will lift the curtain a little to show the Garter Room turned into a cinema or turn back the carpets in the Great Hall to reveal a badminton court. Then the politicians will no longer dare abuse the symbols of monarchy because the laugh will be on them.

CHRISTOPHER OWEN

Christopher Owen was born in Bulawayo, in 1941. A third generation Rhodesian, his family originally settled in Rhodesia about 1900. Educated at Christian Brothers College, Bulawayo he studied law before being commissioned into the Rhodesian Army. He was posted to the 1st Battalion The Rhodesian African Rifles and resigned his commission after UDI. In May 1965 he was appointed Aide-de-Camp and Personal Assistant to the Governor of Rhodesia.

A QUESTION OF LOYALTY

CHRISTOPHER OWEN

It is my sincere conviction that the oath of loyalty to the monarch is supremely binding. A matter of principle, reinforced by deep sentiment and tradition, and confirmed by a solemn undertaking before God, it is an uncompromising contract. To break it is firstly a moral transgression, and secondly an act of personal dishonour.

Many people will argue that this is too sweeping a statement. I would agree at once that there are obvious limitations. Fundamental changes in the monarchial complex – such as the rise of a Nero, regal insanity, or the coronation of another 'Bad King John' – may alter the whole position. A scrupulously carried-out change of national structure through the expressed wish of a substantial majority of all citizens would also be such a case. In these instances, however, the transition of loyalties is usually a smooth, virtually painless operation. It is normally sanctioned by popular approval and ordinary common sense. No extraordinary or outrageous adjustment is required by the individual.

Sometimes, however, a set of circumstances arises which involves the personal integrity of an individual and places him in the unenviable position of having to choose between conflicting loyalties. I have presumably been invited to write this essay, not because of any outstanding literary or rhetorical skills – I do not pretend to have any – but because I found myself in just such a dilemma. On November 11, 1965, the then legal government of Rhodesia declared a political change which clashed with my oath of allegiance to the Queen. A Rhodesian citizen, I was at that time an officer in the Rhodesian Army. I subsequently resigned my commission. It does not fall within my brief to discuss here either the wisdom or justice of the government's declaration, or my own actions. It is mentioned, however, to ensure that the reader understands the point of view from which this essay was written. The fact that I write from personal experience may for some readers confirm, and for others invalidate, the genuiness of my convictions.

Over the centuries the monarchy has come to exemplify those principles and ideals which form the basis of behaviour in our community. The monarch stands for integrity, public service and, above all, loyalty. He is the custodian of a nation's values, and it is a situation accepted by his subjects. Indeed they demand it of him. Commoners, being only frail human beings, may fall short of perfection, but monarchs must constantly maintain the highest of standards.

We are conditioned, as is he, to the moment of coronation. This is his predestined task – to accept the crown, and with it all the duties, obligations and weary works that make it the heaviest of burdens. It is unthinkable that he might refuse it. The words from the *Order of Coronation* are explicit: 'Sirs, I here present unto you QUEEN ELIZABETH your undoubted Queen. Wherefore, all you who are come this day to do your homage and service, are you willing to do the same?' The monarch, it seems, has little discretion in the matter. To decline would be to abdicate not merely the throne, but also to betray all the fundamental values given into his guard. And how quickly shocked the nation becomes should he slip, be it ever so momentarily, from the peoples' pedestal of virtue. The Duke of Edinburgh may play polo on Sunday, but he must be prepared to find the columns of Monday's newspapers choked with a hundred letters of protest from old ladies with convulsions. It is not difficult (although one may not agree with their viewpoint) to understand these accusatory cries. A particular sense of the proprietaries has been offended; by the husband of the person into whose hands those hundred old ladies deposited their ideals on Sunday observance for safeguard.

This peculiarly personal relationship between the British monarch and his peoples is I think typified in an accedote recalled by David Duff in his book *Mother of the Queen*. He tells of an incident during the last war, when King George VI was on one of his numerous visits to the badly blitzed East End of London. As the royal car was leavng the area a man seized hold of an equerry's arm, and pointing at the King said: 'You see him? That's why we sing "There'll always be an England". God bless him!' The cynic might say that this was just a further example of the sentimental emotionalism that always tends to surround the throne. If so, it is nevertheless also an indication of how successful the Royal Family have been in carrying out what might almost have been thought an impossible task. The British monarchy has built itself a reputation that is today almost inviolable. Nor has it been built on loose foundations. Its position has been assured, not by its appeal to sentiment and false pomp, but by hard work, dedication, and a profound loyalty to all the nations which it heads.

Loyalty is the essence without which no social organization could properly function. The phenomenon which ultimately binds the individual to the group, and the group to the individual, it is the reality behind the 'family unit'. By apparent evolution it makes possible the political entities of province, nation, and family of nations. An illustration of this might be found in the over-simplified instruction given to newly-joined army recruits: the soldier is loyal to his section, which is loyal to the platoon, in turn loyal to the company, which belongs wholeheartedly to the regiment. In a single word, therefore, loyalty means unity. It has, in fact, been the *sine qua non* of community living since the days of the cave man. Because loyalty is a spiritual experience of a deeply personal nature, man cannot be forced to fix it unwillingly. It is a voluntary avowal. At the same time society may rightly expect that once a loyalty has been affirmed the individual will abide by it.

The magic of the crown, however, is that here and here alone is an individual born already dedicated to his loyalty. The monarch alone has no real choice – only death or abdication provides the way out. Not so the republican president whose election to office is actively sought by himself. No democratic republic acclaims the birth of one of its citizens and watches him grow to maturity in the confident expectation of eventually swearing him in as its leader. The heir to a throne, on the other hand, is constantly exposed to a clutching public from the day of his birth. This is as it should be. The monarch belongs to his people. But it is also right that he should expect and receive a reciprocating loyalty from his subjects. I think it was Arthur Bryant who wrote that a decent respect for the throne is a sign of good citizenship. The Queen surely deserves more from her people? It may be fashionable to deride the Establishment, but to me it always seems that those writers who so consistently attack the Queen personally and the British monarchy in general show a trace of cowardness in doing so. It is a furtive, rather sly, business to assault a person who is not only powerless to defend himself in public controversy, but has little say regarding his destiny.

While the task of defending a nation's morals is important, it does not end there. The Queen's role today – far more encompassing, far more arduous in its complexities, than that of her predecessors – is a vital one in the establishment of the Commonwealth. And what an extraordinary proposition this latter is! At first glance it seems almost presumptuous to expect even the faintest of harmony from such a hotch-potch of republics, democracies and dictatorships, aspirations, creeds and colours. Only a powerful influence could have held together so heterogeneous a group of nations. It is not unreasonable to suppose that the crown has provided the cohesive factor.

Despite the many thousands of miles that separate him, the colonial – though nobody seems to like that word anymore – is often more ardent, and more artless, in his royalist fervour than the Londoner living a few hundred yards from Buckingham Palace. To him the crown is still a symbol of majesty. It has the power still to provide a very genuine and sincere inspiration to millions of people – to many of whom the Queen is little more than a glossy photograph on the front of a magazine. Perhaps it is because of this that her influence is still so great. Familiarity has not had time to breed cynical indifference. The magic has never quite worn off. In the older Commonwealth countries at least, there is a carefully nurtured belief in the idealized concept of the monarchy. In the past no royal occasion was ever more enthusiastically celebrated than in some dusty far-flung outpost of the British Empire. The tradition – maintained and cherished – lives on. When I first went to England I was horrified at the casual way in which cinema-goers walked out of a theatre while the Anthem was being played. In Rhodesia this would have been taboo, regarded as an insult not only to Her Majesty but to the country. It would have earned the offender probably a censorious lecture from his neighbours. and possibly protest of a more violent nature!

Today, of course, there is something of a new order in Rhodesia. The country has experienced a social upheaval from which she may find it difficult to recover. Many of her citizens, bedevilled by the propaganda of both her own and Britain's politicians, have become disillusioned by the seeming impotence of the monarch. 'But why doesn't the Queen do something?' is a cry often heard in Rhodesia today. It is perhaps an indication of how deeply the colonial regards his monarch. He is literally unable to grasp the constitutional issues of the monarchy because he has been brought up to think of the sovereign in the light of complete omnipotence. What happens, therefore, when the government of a country declares its independence from Britain and supplants the Queen's representative? The certain result is confusion, unhappiness and bewilderment in the minds of all reasonable and responsible citizens. By some strange alchemy those principles which have served so well in the past are suddenly confounded, and each individual is faced with the impossible task of choosing between his country and his Queen. Only yesterday the two were indissoluble.

Perhaps no one outside the country can really appreciate the full extent of the struggle that must be going on in the minds of thousands of Rhodesians today. The judge, the commissioned army officer, the police constable, the civil service clerk – how do they feel? They have all sworn loyalty to the Queen, but they are also Rhodesians. In this most difficult of mental conflicts there is no one to whom they may turn for advice or help. This is a matter for the individual conscience. Often a tedious affair, when it differs with a government's policies, a conscience can become positively dangerous. But whatever the 'official' decision may turn out to be, many Rhodesians will remain loyal to the Queen for a long time to come.

Old traditions and habits die hard, and when the habit is fortified by a sworn testimonial it is that much harder to kill. Any man who cares for his personal honour does not break an oath made before God, or discard a basic principle simply because he is ordered to do so. To fight against the current of popular feeling is not an easy thing to do, but only the gutless reject an ideal because they are told to by other men. A great leader once said that if a thing was worth living for, it was worth dying for. It sounds trite because it has been said in many different ways before, by many other people. Perhaps the poet expressed it best when he said:

'Self-reverence, self-knowledge, self-control,
These three alone lead life to sovereign power.'

Disloyalty, especially on a national scale, breeds anarchy. Disloyalty to the monarch cuts deep at the very roots of our system of government. It is the crown which provides unity and continuity to Britain and the Commonwealth. Equity, personal sentiment, religious scruples – leave all these aside, and it is this requisite to continuity surely that finally must dictate our convictions. We need the monarchy, as surely as a ship needs an anchor. Sir Winston Churchill recognized this ultimate purpose, and made it plain when he told the Commons: 'Above the ebb and flow of party strife, the rise and fall of ministries and individuals, the changes of public opinion or public fortune, the British monarchy presides, ancient, calm and supreme within its function, over all the treasures that have been saved from the past and all the glories we write in the annals of our country.'

SIMON RAVEN

Simon Raven was born in 1927 and educated at Charter-house and King's College, Cambridge. He became a prize-man in 1949 (Members' English Essay Prize), gradu-ated with an honours degree in Classics in 1951, and was a research student between 1951 and 1952. He was a regular officer in the King's Shropshire Light Infantry between 1953 and 1957, serving in Germany from 1953 to 1955, and in Kenya as a Company Commander from 1955 to 1956. He resigned in 1957. Since then he has been a full-time writer, writing novels, plays for radio and television, reviews and essays for *The Observer, Spectator, New Statesman, Punch, Encounter* and other periodicals.

PUBLICATIONS:

Novels: *The Feathers of Death; Brother Cain; Doctors Wear Scarlet; Close of Play; Alms for Oblivion* (a series of ten novels) consisting to date of *The Rich Pay Late, Friends in Low Places, The Sabre Squadron,* and *Fielding Gray.* Essays: 'The English Gentleman'; 'Boys Will be Boys'. Television Plays: *The Scapegoat; The Gaming Book; A Pyre for Private James; A Soirée At Blossoms Hotel; Royal Foundation.*

A MONARCH FOR ME

SIMON RAVEN

I am a royalist. As a young soldier, over twenty years ago, I swore an oath of loyalty to His Majesty King George VI, his heirs and successors. I have eaten his salt, and I have eaten that of the present monarch, and the oath is quite irrevocable: I am the Queen's man, and there is an end of it.

What is more, I am very glad to be. I accept the Queen, with pleasure and conviction, as the latest in a line of legitimate sovereigns who have ruled this country for over 900 years. Nor do I consider that she is merely a symbol representative of the nation or people: she is the supreme head of her kingdom, and it is by her authority that our laws are enacted and our government is conducted. In the Army I obeyed the orders of my superiors because the sovereign commanded me to do so; for no other reason at all. By the same token I now obey (more or less) the government in power, not because it has been elected by the people, but because it has been recognized by the Queen. As far as I am concerned, its edicts go out, not in the name of democracy or social justice or Harold Wilson, but in the name of the Queen, who has seen fit to ratify the decisions of her two Houses of Parliament being duly assembled. I am sorry that some of these edicts are quite so foolish, but if they are good enough for Her Majesty's assent they must be good enough for mine.

And furthermore, if the Queen says that such or such a man is to be a knight or a peer of the realm, and that being so he is my social superior and may take precedence of me, then he *is* my social superior and I am happy to yield him the *pas*. I remember, at the same time, that the Queen also says that I myself, by virtue of office formerly held in her service, am an esquire and therefore entitled to take precedence of all mere gentlemen, yeomen, artisans and labourers. I am *their* superior, and I see no reason why they should resent it, any more than I resent being socially inferior (as I freely admit I am) to a Companion of the Bath or even an MBE. So far from being a proper matter for resentment, this makes things very much simpler and clearer: I know my exact place in the social scheme of things, and if only everybody else did too the nation's business – that is, the Queen's business – would go ahead a great deal faster.

And again: the Queen is head of the Church of England, and for that reason, although I believe Christianity to be a pack of lies and nonsense, I am prepared to accept the Church of England for formal and official purposes. (If the Queen has the sense she seems to have, that is all *she* will be accepting it for.) I am happy to describe myself as 'C. of E.' (rather than make a pedantic fuss) and to attend occasional rituals, which are often very prettily got up. Out of courtesy to the Queen, I acknowledge the social standing of her bishops and the rest; and although I reserve the right to confute their doctrines in print, I should not dream of pulling down their palaces or making a scene in their cathedrals or their churches. As they have, in any case, too much sense to bother me with claims of spiritual authority, I am delighted to accord them temporal respect. It might appear to some that my atheism is in conflict with my loyalty to 'God's anointed', but this is not the case; for to me the religious sanction is unimportant when I consider that Her Majesty has so massive an historical and legal sanction behind her. Nor does the fact of my being an unbeliever mean that the oath, to which I referred earlier, was bogus; for although I swore by a God in whom I did not and do not believe, I also regarded myself as swearing in the name of fealty and honour.

But surely, my reader may urge, you must find that your position is *politically* a little difficult . . . in an age when equality and human rights are so widely and earnestly canvassed? As to equality, the answer is simple: I have already made it quite clear above that I do not believe in it and am not concerned with it; I *want* to be unequal – to be able to look up and to look down – if only because an equal society, like any other plane surface, must be a bore. And as for human rights, I am sick of the sound of them; the more we all think about our rights, the more discontented and greedy we become, and the surest cure for our condition is simply to make the best of what we have got.

There would seem, then, to be nothing whatever to qualify my devotion to the House of Windsor. I am troubled by no problems of politics, religion, conscience, authority, provenance or degree. However, there is just one awkward snag. You see, the kind of loyalty I advocate and would desire to offer is personal, individual; my loyalty, like that of all true royalists, is not that of an obedient citizen to an abstraction or a symbol, but that of one person to another. I do not expect (or even particularly want) to be afforded a physical encounter with the monarch, but I would wish, on the strength of what I hear or read, to admire him or her as much as possible *as a person*.

You begin to see my difficulty, gentle reader?

The one member of the royal house for whom I can feel regard at this moment is the Queen Mother: the sight of her bouncing round National Hunt meetings with such good will and sheer enjoyment has long been enough to ensure that. The rest? Well, they have my most sincere respect and duty, yet I cannot feel for them that private affection which is based, *not* necessarily on actual acquaintance, but on tastes known to be shared, or a presence seen – even distantly or on television – to be pleasing, or a sympathetic attitude widely reported, or even (whisper it) reputed moral weaknesses. I cannot feel the true affection, warm all through even where disillusioned, which lies, for example, behind this passage of Sir Edmund Varney:

'You have satisfaction in your conscience that you are in the right; that the King ought not to grant what is required of him; and so you do your duty and your business together: but for my part I do not like the quarrel, and do heartily wish that the King would yield and consent to what they desire; so that my conscience is only concerned in honour and gratitude to follow my master. I have eaten his bread, and served him near thirty years, and will not do so base a thing as to forsake him; and choose rather to lose my life (which I am sure I shall do) to preserve and defend those things which are against my conscience to preserve and defend . . .'

Whenever I read this passage, I ask myself, what is it about the Royal Family which, for me at least, limits their appeal and makes my response to them, while it is correct enough, a mere formality – something infinitely weaker and less real than what was felt by stout Sir Edmund, who was prepared to damn his conscience in order to serve his prince? Why, I ask myself, cannot I feel like that about the Queen, her husband, and the heir apparent, her son?

The answer is, I think, that in each case there is something that they lack. The Queen herself is a sensible and dignified woman, by no means without charm, who has worked conscientiously at a thankless job; and yet I can feel no strong bond, because spontaneity is lacking. It is impossible to imagine that she should lose her temper, or giggle, or suddenly say something quite outrageous. And so it is with Prince Philip and Prince Charles.

If only they were not so middle-class in public aspect and attitude. Prince Philip, it is true, breaks out orally from time to time, but he does so in the safe *persona* of the bluff no-nonsense sailor, in whom a little licence is traditionally acceptable. His sallies and his jokes are mere wardroom currency, in no way repudiating, if anything emphasizing, the *bourgeois* image of his role; for after the second or at most the third pink gin, he will merely step ashore and return to a domestic supper. If only he would stay out all night and wind up on a drunk charge in Bow Street, how much more he might appeal.

Or consider Prince Charles. Picture him in his rooms, in the most beautiful court in the most beautiful university in the world. The surroundings are ideal for one or both of two pursuits; that of learning (as the clock tells the peaceful hours, and the fountain murmurs, and the ghost of Master Bentley paces with unheard tread); or that of pleasure, for which so noble and elegant a scene would make an unrivalled background and to which Charles might bring all the relish of his youth. Either pursuit would be understood and applauded by the ghosts that linger and by all of us who ever heard the chimes at midnight, over book or over bottle. A princely place, one would think, for a prince to enlighten and disport himself, to entertain the wise by day and to fête the young and the beautiful by night, to surround himself with wit and laughter and put on shows and revelries and masques . . . Yet one knows that none of this will happen. The two years in the Great Court of Trinity will pass in the ingestion of decorous half-truths (nothing original or dangerous or deep), while perhaps three or four sedate little parties, carefully calculated to give offence to no one, will be arranged by aides for a tightly closed and totally respectable circle of friends. No gaiety, no colour, no adventure: for what would the Palace say?

It is not the Queen's fault, of course. She has been rigidly brought up to know what is required of her, which is to set an example of chastity and self-discipline, to nod gracious approval of all the nation's more necessary and tedious activities, and occasionally to trot out a discreet selection of platitudes in order to convince the bored and average citizen that he is the salt of the earth. With such a function as this to perform, she cannot afford to tamper with the proprieties or allow much latitude to her eldest son. But what I could wish is that she would look less contented with it all; what I could wish is that every now and again a smile of irony or a positive snarl of contempt would pass over her face, as if to say, 'I know this is a bloody sham, I know these people are toadies, malingerers and hypocrites, and I wish to hell I could say so.'

On the contrary, however, the Queen is at perennial pains to suppress all her most restless and critical instincts. If only one Christmas day after luncheon perhaps, they would suddenly come bursting out, how delighted one would be. But can anyone even begin to imagine such a scene? Is it conceivable that the adamantine discipline should ever crack?

In short, my burden is this: the Queen though head of a nation which once ruled the world and has produced the finest literature and the most resounding scandals in history, a nation which is racy, resourceful, bawdy, drunken and deeply poetic withal . . . the Queen, I say, though wearing the crown of such a nation, embodies in her public person and personality only the safest and most stolid qualities of her middle-class subjects. Necessary qualities, admirable qualities, but not qualities which make for love.

And the monarch for me must be a monarch to be loved. Such a monarch (I tell myself in hopeful moments) as even Prince Charles might just possibly become if only he would listen to the ghosts in Trinity and read a history book or two. I would have him get the scholarship, but not the pedantry, of James I; the love of experiment, the easy charm, the worldly tolerance of his namesake, Charles II; the spice and fluency of his mother's namesake, Elizabeth I; the exuberance of his grandmother and his grandfather's exquisite manners; the wander-lust of Richard the

Lion-Heart; the style of Edward II and the chivalry of the Black Prince; the outspokenness of Henry II; the cool courage of Charles I and the beauty of Edward VIII; the fellowship of Prince Hal, the mien of Henry V, the keen appetite of King John, as many wives as Henry VIII and as many mistresses as Edward VII. All these things I wish for him, and the years of Victoria, Queen and Empress, in which to enjoy them. For such a man and such a monarch – civilized, handsome and commanding; lusty, hard-drinking and far-travelled; courteous, sceptical and proud – I would cheerfully go to the block.

Come, come, my reader might well say, enough of these fanciful catalogues. Suppose, just suppose, that Prince Charles did indeed turn out something like you hope – and there *are* good qualities about him – just what good do you suppose it would do? You yourself might love him, as you claim, but everyone else would be at immediate pains to suppress him. For can you not imagine (my reader might continue) the prudishness and the envy, the political suspicions, the sheer outrage of 'democratic and egalitarian susceptibilities', which would be caused at this day and date by the appearance on the throne of a man like that? And if, for the sake of argument, he actually got himself crowned, you know as well as the rest of us that he would only be allowed to reign, never to rule: his life would be that of a constitutional monarch who must go round nodding approval at virtuous factory workers and shaking hands with mayors. The minute he stepped out of line, the minute he started any of this Prince Hal or Charles II stuff, four strong men tastefully got up in gold braid would hustle him into his Rolls and whisk him away to sober up. What you apparently desire (my reader might conclude) is hopelessly out of date and neither needed nor wanted by anyone else at all.

But surely, I might reply, if a monarch were truly loveable, the people would love him. They would pay attention – they would follow his example. And what would his example be? My monarch would be for the arts and against puritanism; he would be a man of accomplishment, not a mere spectator; he would be a man who took risks, not a lover of shameful security; a man who hated ugliness and therefore mistrusted spurious progress; a man sceptical of foolish ideals but always ready to promote, with intelligence and taste, such concrete and pleasurable benefits as time and chance would permit. If the nation took its example from all this . . . instead of the velleity which we have come to associate with royalty . . . then the nation might be much the better for it. Let us have an end of the Welfare Monarchy, for God's sake let us have a KING . . . though I very much fear, gentle reader, that the amiable Prince now incarcerated in Trinity College will not be allowed to turn into quite the monarch for me.

o

NORMAN ST JOHN-STEVAS

Norman St John-Stevas has been Conservative Member of Parliament for Chelmsford since October 1964. He was born in 1929 and educated at Ratcliffe, Fitzwilliam Cambridge, Christ Church Oxford, and Yale. He took first class honours in Law in 1950. He was President of the Cambridge Union in 1950. He has been a lecturer and tutor in law and has won many academic awards in Britain and America. In 1959 he joined the *Economist* to edit the collected works of Walter Bagehot and he became legal, ecclesiastical and political correspondent. He has contributed articles to many other periodicals.

PUBLICATIONS:
Obscenity and the Law, 1956; *Walter Bagehot*, 1959; *Life, Death and the Law*, 1961; *The Right to Life*, 1963; *Law and Morals*, 1964; *The Literary Works of Walter Bagehot*, 1965; *The Historical Works of Walter Bagehot*, 1967; *The Agonizing Choice*, 1969.

THE MONARCHY AND
THE PRESENT

NORMAN ST JOHN-STEVAS

The two most venerable institutions of the western world are the papacy and the British monarchy and they have much in common. Both rely for much of their influence on arousing reverence and awe: neither has in practice great executive power: continuity is essential for both. Queen Victoria, who had great prescience about the foundations of her own position, saw the community of interest: when Pio Nono lost his temporal power, she was quite definitely not amused.

In my view the principal functions of the monarchy today are symbolic and religious although the monarch has certain constitutional functions as well. In a sense the monarchy should not have to explain itself but in a utilitarian age this cannot be avoided altogether. Ignoring Bagehot's precept some daylight does have to be let in upon magic. The relevance of the monarchy to the country today is that the monarch symbolizes the nation. The Queen has to represent both the contemporary life of the nation and its historic past, a dual function which can cause conflict. The monarchy must change with the times and symbolize the present national aspirations: to become a museum piece would be fatal: yet at the same time an essential function of the monarch is to remind the country that there is more to the nation than the present generation and to link it both with the past and with the future. By assuming this role of national symbol the monarchy strengthens the nation. In Britain, however fierce the party strife, no citizen ever has to be against the country. The difference in this respect between ourselves and the United States, for example, is marked. There, because the president is both a symbolic embodiment of the country and a partisan figure, one half of the nation finds itself in the embarrassing position of appearing to be opposed to the aspirations of the country when in fact they are merely rejecting the nominee of a particular party. The loyalty which constellates round the monarch in Britain finds a centre in the United States in the flag, but an abstract piece of bunting is no substitute for a symbol of flesh and blood. Countries which separate the head of the executive from the head of the state by artificial means do not fare much better, since the president is either an extremely dim and shadowy figure or, if not, tends to become a focus of political divisiveness instead of national unity.[1] This is not to say that I believe that monarchy is suitable for every country or that monarchy on the British model can be exported. One should simply recognize that for historical and other reasons the British nation has an almost unique natural advantage in its monarchical constitution.

The British monarchy is in one sense a conservative force but by this very fact it in fact facilitates change. A nation has two basic needs, that for stability and that for change, and the monarchy by preserving the idea of continuity in the life of the country enables it to absorb more radical changes in its political and social structure than would otherwise be possible without real risk or disorder. It moderates the bitterness of party strife by providing a focus of loyalty which is common to all parties in the state and by judicious intervention it can at a time of extreme party conflict be an effective moderating influence, as was shown on a number of occasions during the reign of King George V. Similar circumstances might well arise in the future.

The monarchy symbolizes not only the political life of the nation but its moral and religious life as well. This, of course, has not always been so. The Stuart kings by their Laudian Anglicanism and Roman Catholicism repelled many and, until the accession of Queen Victoria, the Hanoverian dynasty did not exactly provide a model of domestic rectitude; but Queen Victoria and in particular her successors George V and George VI imparted a moral force to the monarchy which has been maintained by the present Queen. Indeed this aspect of the monarchy is more important than ever today when both the established Church and nonconformity are in decline. The association of monarchy with religion strengthens both.[2] Again in a society

---

[1] The whole world knows who is Queen of England, but how many people could name the present President of Germany?

[2] Under the Constitution it is a condition of title to the Crown that the sovereign should 'join in communion with the Church of England as by law established'. Under the Bill of Rights and Act of Settlement, succession to the throne is restricted to Protestants and, Catholics are specifically

which has grown steadily more permissive (a process which is both good and bad) the example of a united family life set by the Queen, her husband, children, and her close relations is a real contribution to the nation's morality. The influence of the crown, declared Disraeli in 1872, 'is not confined merely to political affairs. England is a domestic country. Here the home is revered and the hearth sacred. The nation is represented by a family – the Royal Family; and if that family is educated with a sense of responsibility and a sentiment of public duty, it is difficult to exaggerate the salutary influence they may exercise over a nation.' Today one might not express the idea in quite the same language but in itself it is as true as it was when Disraeli uttered it a hundred years ago.

The English monarch is of course a constitutional sovereign but that is a very different thing from being a cypher. The best description of the general constitutional rights of the sovereign is still that given by Bagehot in his *English Constitution*, 'the right to be consulted, the right to encourage, the right to warn'. These rights grow in effectiveness as the reign lengthens and the monarch acquires a fund of experience which none of his ministers can match. Already the Queen has a much wider personal knowledge of the working of the constitution in times of stress than any possible prime minister. As she is assiduous in her political duties and follows parliamentary life closely and sees

excluded. The sovereign may not be married to a Catholic. These provisions are open to objection on two grounds:

(1) they discriminate against Catholics.
(2) they derogate from the basic human rights of the sovereign and infringe his religious liberty.

These objections are theoretically valid, but the relation of crown and Church is the creation of history, not logic. As long as the royal supremacy over the Church is retained and the sovereign remains 'supreme governor' of the Church, obligatory membership of the Church of England is not unreasonable. On the other hand, the provisions *explicitly* excluding Catholics from the succession to the throne might with advantage be done away with. If the Church were to be separated from the state and the royal supremacy abolished then the case for doing away with the restrictions on the sovereign's religion would be greatly strengthened. At the same time it should be recognized that it is probably an advantage to have a Protestant sovereign (Anglican in England, Presbyterian in Scotland) as the United Kingdom is largely Protestant and a Catholic monarch would be separated by religion from the majority of his subjects.

her prime minister at regular intervals her advice must always be taken seriously.

Apart from this general function of wise and impartial adviser the monarch can and has been an important moderating influence in specific crises. In July 1914 King George V held a conference of leading politicians at Buckingham Palace to see if a moderate settlement on the Irish issue could be secured. Again during the general strike of 1926 the King exerted his influence to secure a reasonable settlement. He played an important but wholly constitutional role in the formation of the National Government in 1931. In the present precarious economic state of Britain this aspect of the monarch's role might well emerge again. If for example the devaluation measures fail to achieve their object a coalition might be the only alternative left for Britain and the Queen could play an important part in bringing this about.

Quite apart from these generalized powers the Queen retains a number of personal prerogatives which can be exercised in her own right and without the intervening advice of her ministers. The choice of prime minister is still in theory the Queen's but situations can and have arisen where she exercises an effective personal choice. Bagehot recognized two situations where the crown had a personal choice of prime minister, first where no one party commands a clear majority, and second where the majority party possesses no recognized leader. Both of these situations could still arise today. Suppose for example at the next general election the two major parties were almost equally balanced and the Liberals held the balance of power; in the course of subsequent manoeuvrings the choice of the Queen might well be decisive. The second exception is now more unlikely to arise as all the parties now have arrangements for electing their own leaders by ballot of the parliamentary party. Nevertheless if a prime minister died in office, especially a Conservative prime minister, the Queen might well be called on to make a selection which could greatly influence the outcome of any subsequent party election.[1]

[1] In the event of the death or resignation of the prime minister while in office the practice followed in Australia might possibly commend itself for English use. When Mr A. J. Lyons, Australian Prime Minister,

The second sphere for the exercise of a personal prerogative is that of the dissolution of parliament. Can the monarch dissolve parliament without the advice of the prime minister? My own view is negative. She might however be able to proceed in the following manner. She could request her prime minister to advise a dissolution and on his refusal invite another to form a government who would proffer the necessary advice. The right to dissolve would thus be dependent on the sovereign's ability to find someone willing to form an alternative government. Inevitably however the crown would be plunged into party conflict and its occurrence is extremely improbable. If however the Queen cannot dissolve parliament can she refuse to grant a dissolution? Normally she cannot although Queen Victoria zealously maintained that she could, yet even she never in practice refused a dissolution. In November 1918 King George V tried to dissuade Lloyd George from dissolving and took the same course with Baldwin in 1923 but in each case the request was eventually granted. In October 1924 the King was very unwilling to grant Ramsay MacDonald a dissolution and only conceded it when he had established by conversations with both opposition leaders that they were unwilling to form a government. The position then would seem to be that despite the absence of any refusal for over a hundred years, the prime minister has no absolute right to a dissolution, the the sovereign can dispense with his advice if he can find an alternative prime minister. The danger of this course is that the second minister may be defeated

died in office in 1939, the United Australian Party which he headed possessed no deputy leader. The Governor-General called on the leader of the Country Party and deputy Prime Minister to form a caretaker government until the U.A.P. elected a successor to Mr Lyons. Sir Earle Page who had been selected resigned nineteen days later when Mr Menzies was elected U.A.P.Leader. Similar action was taken some years later when Mr Curtin died in office. Mr Forde, deputy Labour party leader, held office for six days until the Labour party met and elected Mr J. B. Chifley as leader. Mr Forde was an unsuccessful candidate in the ballot. This procedure was again followed in 1967. Mr. Holt, the Australian Prime Minister, was accidentally drowned in December 1967. Mr McEwen then took over as acting Prime Minister. Mr John Gorton was elected leader of the Liberal Party and thereupon took office as Prime Minister. Cf: A similar procedure was followed in India on the death of Mr Nehru in 1964 and of Mr Shastri in 1966.

and the sovereign obliged to grant to the second what he had refused to the first.[1]

A third area of personal prerogative concerns the creation of peers: 'the safety valve' of the constitution by which the executive can if necessary overcome the resistance of the Upper House. The monarch cannot on his own initiative make a wholesale creation of peers to swamp the Upper House but he can do so constitutionally if acting on the advice of his prime minister. However he is not *bound* to do so and in the exercise of his right of refusal discretion becomes important. Ultimately he must judge for himself whether the political situation is sufficiently grave to justify so serious a step.

The last of the sovereign's personal prerogatives is concerned with patronage and the conferment of honours. The sovereign is the fount of honours but honours today with few exceptions are conferred on the advice of the prime minister. The sovereign may refuse to grant an honour but nowadays this is rare. Queen Victoria in fact refused to admit John Bright to the Privy Council in 1859: declined to admit Sir Leopold de Rothschild to the peerage in 1869 and Sir Garnet Wolseley in 1881. The Royal Victorian Order is awarded personally by the crown and – since December 1946 – the orders of the Garter and the Thistle. The prime minister's advice is not required for an award of the Order of Merit.

From time to time it has been suggested that the crown possesses a veto, namely the right to refuse consent to legislation that has passed both Houses of Parliament. Such a veto has not

[1] This situation actually arose in Canada in 1926. In September 1925 Mr Mackenzie King requested a dissolution from the Governor-General, Lord Byng, which was granted. His Conservative opponents, led by Mr Meighen gained a majority of fifteen, but the Liberals remained in office, supported by the Labour party. In June 1926, after a vote of censure, he requested a dissolution, but was refused by Lord Byng, first because Mr Meighen's party being the largest single party in the chamber should be given a chance of forming a government and secondly because it would mean a second general election within nine months. Mr Meighen thereupon formed a government, was defeated three days later by one vote and requested a dissolution. This time the request was granted but a Liberal majority was returned. Lord Byng was severely criticized for his decision. In 1939 Sir Patrick Duncan, Governor-General of South Africa, refused a dissolution to General Hertzog and called upon General Smuts to form a government.

been invoked since the reign of Queen Anne, and its use would only be justified in the most extreme circumstances. Bagehot denied that the veto existed and maintained that the Queen must 'sign her own death warrant if the two Houses unanimously send it up to her'. Attempts were made during the home rule crisis immediately before the outbreak of the First World War to get King George V to use his veto on the Home Rule Bill. The King's view on the whole matter is contained in a letter written to Mr Asquith in July 1914 (but never despatched) and is characteristically sane. 'Much has been said and written in favour of the proposition that the assent of the crown should be witheld from the measure. On the other hand, the King feels strongly that that extreme course should not be adopted in this case unless there is convincing evidence that it would avert a national disaster, or at least have a tranquilizing effect on the distracting conditions of the time. There is no such evidence.'[1] Probably the only justification for the use of the veto would be an attempt by a government to destroy the democratic basis of the constitution, such as the sponsoring of a bill (at a time other than one of national emergency) to prolong the life of parliament indefinitely. The difficulty is that once exercised imprudently the use of the veto would bring the monarchy itself to an end.

Apart from the exercise of constitutional rights at home, the crown has an important constitutional and symbolic role in the Commonwealth overseas. The members of the British Commonwealth, declared the Statute of Westminster (1931), are a free association of nations, 'united by a common allegiance to the crown'. Full legislative autonomy was conferred on the dominion parliaments, and after the passing of the statute, no law passed by the parliament of the United Kingdom was to extend to any dominion without its express request and consent, declared in the relevant Act. A further development came in 1949 when the crown became the symbol of India's membership of the Commonwealth, but surrendered all prerogative powers. In April 1949 the Conference of Commonwealth Prime Ministers issued the following statement:

'The government of India have informed the other govern-

[1] Royal Archives, K. 2553 VI. 56.

ments of the Commonwealth of the intention of the Indian people that under the new constitution which is about to be adopted India shall become a sovereign and independent republic. The government of India have, however, declared and affirmed India's desire to continue her full membership of the Commonwealth of Nations and her acceptance of the King as the symbol of the free association of its independent member nations and as such the Head of the Commonwealth.'

At that date a number of other nations in the Commonwealth including Pakistan have followed India's lead.

The monarchy, like our other institutions, is not immune from criticism, and in recent years some doubts about its continued utility have been voiced, although there has been nothing equivalent to the republican movement which grew up in England in the 1860s. Led by Charles Bradlaugh, it commanded support at various times from men such as Dilke, Joseph Chamberlain, Bright and John Morley. In 1871 the movement was stimulated by the proclamation of the French Republic, but the illness of the Prince of Wales, and the subsequent outburst of popular rejoicing on his recovery finished the movement as an effective force.

It is sometimes argued that the hereditary principle is not supportable in any institution playing a prominent role in a modern state. This theoretical objection is reinforced in practice by the argument that it involves a lottery in genetics and sooner or later a losing ticket is bound to be drawn. Bagehot's criticism was sharp:

'A constitutional sovereign must in the common course of government be a man of but common ability. I am afraid, looking to the early acquired feebleness of hereditary dynasties, that we must expect him to be a man of inferior ability. Theory and experience both teach that the education of a prince can be but a poor education and that a royal family will generally have less ability than other families. What right then have we to expect the perpetual entail on any family of an exquisite discretion, which if it be not a sort of genius, is at least as rare as genius?'

The hereditary principle is however quite defensible both in theory and in practice. The basic unit of our society remains the family and so long as this is so the Royal Family is not so much an anomaly as an apotheosis. In any case what more acceptable alternative is there? An elective monarchy has grave drawbacks not least that it would open the highest position in the country to competition. This would increase the scramble for social distinction which is moderated by the hereditary character of the monarchy. The English are a theatrical people and care about the show and would be eager to take part in it. If the highest post in conspicuous life were thrown open to public competition, wrote Bagehot, 'this low sort of ambition and envy would be fearfully increased. Politics would offer a prize too dazzling for mankind; clever base people would strive for it and stupid base people would envy it.' In a society which is becoming increasingly a mobile and competitive meritocracy there is value in preserving an institution whose hereditary basis points to another scale of values.

As to the danger of producing unsuitable monarchs this simply has not happened to the British monarchy in modern times. Queen Victoria, Edward VII, George V, George VI, and Queen Elizabeth II, have all served the country well. The only controversial figure has been that of Edward VIII and he proved willing to vacate the throne rather than threaten in any way the continuance of the monarchy. Clearly, however, the education of the heir to the throne, becomes of very great importance in an hereditary system, to ensure that as much is done as possible to fit him for his eventual sovereign role. The question of how the heir to the throne is educated is one that falls within the royal prerogative and the prime minister of the day is not normally consulted officially although his views may well be sought unofficially by the monarch. When the question of the Prince of Wales's children going on a world cruise was discussed by the Cabinet in 1879 and objections lodged, the Queen protested strongly and Lord Beaconsfield agreed that the matter should not have been brought before the Cabinet. Whether the education of the present Prince of Wales has been entirely suitable for his character is a matter of some doubt, as it appears to have been of somewhat too extrovert and 'hearty' a character for a boy who has wide intellectual and aesthetic interests, but it has certainly been of a much more 'normal' character than that of any previous heir to the throne. Attendance at a public school instead of the employment of a private tutor was undoubtedly a wise step although whether Gordonstoun was the right school is open to question. Again the period at Timbertop in Australia was a good idea but it might well be supplemented by attendance at a later stage at a continental or American university. The decision to send Prince Charles to Cambridge and in particular to allow him to lead as 'normal' a life as possible was also wise. The mistake of attempting to cloister away a young man of spirit and vigour from the life of the university, which was made in the case of Edward VII, is evidently not to be repeated.

A further hazard that faces the heir to the throne is the possibility of an extended period of idleness as the result of a preceding long reign. Today however when royal etiquette has become much more relaxed there is much greater scope for the heir to the throne to find a satisfying and useful occupation if he so desires. Much of Prince Charles's time will doubtless be spent in travel but this is not incompatible with the pursuit of a profession or other definite activity, should this be his wish. Clearly the heir to the throne has to give fairly close attention to politics both national and international if he is eventually to discharge his role of constitutional sovereign satisfactorily. What is true of the heir is also true of other members of the Royal Family close to the succession to the throne. The possibility of their accession cannot be ignored. The eight monarchs who have reigned since 1800 were in only five cases, George IV, Edward VII, Edward VIII and Elizabeth II, direct heirs to the throne. George V and George VI were both second sons. Accordingly the education of all those who have a tangible possibility of succeeding to the throne should take this fact into account.

A favourite charge which opponents of the monarchy level against it is that it is an expensive and extravagant institution. How justified is this? The first point to note is that only certain members of the Royal Family receive any support from public funds, namely the Queen, the Duke of Edinburgh, their children, Princess Margaret, the Queen Mother and the Duke of Gloucester. The principal source of the public income of the sovereign is the Civil List which is voted by parliament at the beginning of each reign. The present Civil List is made up as follows: Privy Purse (personal spending) £60,000; Household Salaries £185,000; Household Expenses £121,800; Royal Bounty (for the support of charities) £13,200; Supplementary Provision

£95,000 (designed to take account of inflation), making a grand total of £475,000. This is considerably less than the Civil List granted to King George VI which amounted to £410,000, at a time when money values were considerably higher than they are today. Payments to other members of the Royal Family are charged on the consolidated fund. They are as follows: the Queen Mother £70,000, the Duke of Edinburgh £40,000, Princess Margaret £15,000, the Duke of Gloucester £35,000. Princess Anne and any other daughters of the Queen are entitled to £6,000 per year at twenty-one, which is increased to £15,000 on marriage. Sons of the sovereign other than the heir to the throne receive £10,000 a year at twenty-one, which becomes £25,000 a year on marriage. Pensions to members of the royal household are chargeable to the consolidated fund.

In addition to the Civil List income, the sovereign or the heir to the throne are entitled to the income of the Duchies of Lancaster and Cornwall. The net income of the Duchy of Lancaster for 1963-4 (the last year for which figures are available) was £160,000, and this was paid to the Queen. The net income for the Duchy of Cornwall for the same period was £169,665 and the arrangements for its disposition are somewhat more complicated. The Civil List Act provides that the sums due under the Civil List are to be reduced by an amount equal to eight tenths of the income from the Duchy until Prince Charles attains the age of eighteen. Until the Prince is twenty-one the Civil List Act provides that the Civil List shall be reduced by a sum equal to the income of the Duchy less £30,000. On reaching the age of twenty-one, Prince Charles becomes entitled to the whole of the income from the Duchy and no reductions are made in the Civil List.

The Queen is also assisted financially in that the upkeep of a number of the royal palaces is shared with the Ministry of Works, and certain other financial provisions are made by which the expenses of such items as the royal yacht *Britannia* and aircraft of the Queen's Flight are paid for by the government. Other members of the Royal Family are able to use the royal yacht but the Queen requires them to bear any extra expense entailed.

Another fact which should be noted is that at the beginning of the reign the income from the crown estates is surrendered to the Exchequer in return for the Civil List grants. In the financial year ended March 31, 1966, the net income paid into the Treasury from these estates amounted to £3,525,000. Too much need not be made of this but it should be born in mind when making a general assessment of the cost of the monarchy to the nation.

The Queen has her own private fortune made up of her investments, certain private estates such as Sandringham and Balmoral, the royal art collection, etc. The total valuation of this is not known but it would no doubt run into millions, much of it unrealizable in practice. It is sometimes thought that the Queen is not liable to pay income tax but this is not the case. She pays tax on her private income but not on the income from the Duchy of Lancaster which is tax exempt. Other members of the Royal Family pay tax in the normal way. The one tax which the sovereign does escape is estate duty which is not levied on the demise of the crown.

Surveying the available figures it would be absurd to pretend that the British monarchy is cheap but equally it is in no way extravagant. It has a certain splendour and style but that is in accordance with the wishes of a people who like pageantry and pomp. There is something to be said for a splendid monarchy and something to be said for no monarchy but a mean monarchy has nothing to be said for it at all.[1] Royalty on the Scandinavian model would not be popular in England. Furthermore it would be much less attractive to the millions of foreigners who come to England every year attracted in part by the mystique and magnificence of the present monarchy.

Critics of the monarchy unable to find ammunition to fire off against the Queen and rightly aware of the unpopularity of any such course, so great is her hold on the affections of the nation, have turned their fire on other members of the Royal Family and on Princess Margaret in particular, and attempted to make accusations of royal extravagance stick at this level.[2] By her

[1] It is worth noting that the Republican movement grew up in England in the 1860s not because of any ostentation in the court, but because Queen Victoria had virtually withdrawn from public life. The people, in fact, wanted to see more of her, not less.

[2] In fact the consolidated fund provision of £15,000 p.a. for Princess Margaret is far from being excessive when the wide range of her public duties is taken into account. She fulfils more than a hundred public engagements each year. To assist her in her public duties she employs a secretary, two assistants, and a clerk. She also employs a single lady-in-waiting. Lord Snowden receives no income from public funds.

marriage to a commoner Princess Margaret extended the social scope of the Royal Family but at the same time exposed it to a form of sniping from gossip columnists and others from which it had previously been immune. The dangers were pointed out in the *Economist* in a perceptive leading article 'Roses all the way?' of May 7, 1960, on the occasion of the Princess's marriage. But having described the perils the *Economist* proceeded to take a positive view. What, it asked, would the timorous prefer?

'That royalty should not be allowed ordinary contact with any but its own former (but now narrowing) stratum of society? Or that, once it has made broader contacts, it should not be allowed to feel the same emotions as other human beings? The challenge set by the problems surrounding this marriage was threefold. First, to the bridegroom himself, who today strides between two worlds. The world he is leaving is one where ordinary mortals worth their salt guide their actions by their own ideas, enthusiasms, judgements and conceptions of charity – which do not (and, at least among the young, should not) exclude occasional puckish unconventionality and reasonable attachment to the main chance. The world he now enters is one where actions need to be guided much more continuously by an unobtrusive sense of public duty, which is perhaps more easily inherited than explained. But that does not mean that it cannot be assimilated by a young man with *nous*.

'Secondly there will be a challenge after this wedding to the advisers of royalty. They have a special social innovation to handle and there are two pitfalls into which they could fall in the process. One would be foolish to pretend that there is no innovation, and to insist that the new public figure should be made to fit exactly into the orthodox mould. This would be a great mistake, and it is one that traditionalist advisers seem only too liable to make. Is there any real reason, for example, why Princess Margaret's husband should not be allowed in some measure to continue with the artistic profession at which he is skilled, in the same way as Princess Elizabeth's husband at first continued with his naval service? The other mistake would be for royal advisers to take such fright at the innovation as to hide its perpetrators out of sight. If there appeared to be a significant and carefully arranged diminution of the popular Princess's public role, this could have a nationally divisive effect, because by many people it would be resented.

The third challenge is to the press and other organs of public opinion; and here one can only express a hope. It seems appropriate to express it in the same words as the *Economist* used in its closing comments on the last royal wedding. 'When the bells have stopped ringing and the celebrations are over and the crowds are gone, one may hope that to the loyalty and affection which London and the whole Empire have been demonstrating there will be added an element of delicate consideration for that private life to which even Princesses and their consorts are entitled.'

What a hope! Unfair criticism of Princess Margaret started at the time of her wedding and has not ceased since. First it was said that the wedding itself was an unjustified extravagance when in fact the cost of the reception, the honeymoon, and even a percentage of the decorations inside the Abbey was borne by the Queen Mother. Then it was alleged that thousands of pounds of public money had been squandered on Kensington Palace to provide a home for Princess Margaret and her husband. What happened in fact was that after years of neglect by the Ministry of Works a Wren and Kent wing of Kensington Palace, which had been deteriorating since 1929, was restored and saved. The wing had become a derelict, bomb-damaged, dry-rot-ridden dump, but today ranks as a national monument. £120,000 was in fact spent on the restoration, of which £65,000 came from the Ministry of Works. £20,000 was donated personally by the Queen. The Ministry of Works grant was used in the main for necessary structural repairs; all internal decoration and fittings were paid for by the tenants, the interior doors being in fact made by Lord Snowdon. Ultimate beneficiaries of the restoration will be the nation which will have preserved an important part of the palace which otherwise might have been permanently lost. The criticism which centred on this project seems to have been singularly ill founded. The restored house is a comfortable and dignified one in keeping with the position of its occupants but it could in no sense be described as extravagant or ostentatious. The running expenses of the house including the rates of £1,500 are paid for by the Snowdons.

Equally unfair was the criticism made by Mr William Hamilton, MP in the House of Commons in February 1966 of the visit made by the Snowdons to the United States in the previous year.[1] The cost of the visit was £31,000 and details were given in the House of Commons by Mr Walter Padley, Minister of State at the Foreign Office.[2]

The initial mistake was that of the Foreign Office who described it as a 'semi-official' visit, when it was in fact a full official visit, thus opening the way for subsequent criticism. Princess Margaret and her husband were invited originally by the English-Speaking Union to make the visit and during their three weeks in the USA fulfilled over sixty public engagements. During the entire three weeks the couple enjoyed only four days 'off', fulfilling engagements on both Saturdays and Sundays. Publicity perhaps inevitably concentrated on the 'glamour' events such as the visit to Hollywood, and the more humdrum occasions were given less coverage. The success of the visit from the viewpoint of improving Anglo-American relations and benefiting British exports was undoubted. As Mr Padley stated in the House of Commons: 'Many of the press reports praised the Princess and her husband for helping to sell British goods as a result of the royal visit to the shops in Fifth Avenue, twenty-five shops in the week before Christmas displayed British goods. The visit was extremely valuable in furthering the picture which the Americans should have and frequently did not of a modern up-to-date Britain.'[3]

In a letter to *The Times* published in December 1965 Mr Gordon Hearne of California declared: 'The rapport created by this one visit will translate into many millions of dollars of additional purchases of your goods as well as many trips to England by our citizens.' A letter in the *Daily Telegraph* from

[1] Details of the cost were given as follows: £940 advance planning; £9,800 air passages across the Atlantic; £5,000 internal air travel; £4,600 contribution to expenses; £4,000 to hotels etc; £4,000 for official receptions; £2,000 telegraphic communications, printing etc. Figures I have quoted are to the nearest round figure. See *The Times*, February 5, 1966.

[2] During the debate on February 4th in the House of Commons I described Mr Hamilton's attack as 'unchivalrous, petty and mean-minded' and likely to prejudice the beneficial results of the visit.

[3] *The Times*, February 5, 1966.

Mr Leigh Chamberlain of Philadelphia stated: 'Her Royal Highness arrived in the United States prepared to love everyone and everything. Seldom has a visitor been accorded such extensively favourable page one press coverage – and for a non-monarchy we are no strangers to royalty. The Snowdons' visit has engendered untold goodwill for the United Kingdom. They worked hard, meticulously following a schedule that would have crippled many of their detractors.'

Malicious attacks will no doubt continue to pursue Princess Margaret and her husband from time to time in the future, but why? Partly as I have suggested as a means of attacking the monarchy by a side swipe but this is not the entire explanation. Their very accessibility to society has aroused that 'lower sort of ambition and envy' for which Bagehot believed that the English were remarkable. This has been reinforced by the philistinism and puritanism which is never far from the surface of English life and which resents the connection which their marriage has created between the traditionally restricted royal circle and that of the stage, the arts and show business, which to the middle-class Englishman are tainted with the touch of the *demi-monde*.

Apart from alleged extravagance the criticism most often levelled against the crown is that it has failed to change sufficiently rapidly with the times. A picture is built up of a monarch surrounded by a crowd of stuffy courtiers and hemmed in by a small circle of the socially privileged, unrepresentative of modern Britain. Criticism of the Queen's choice of personal friends does not deserve to be treated seriously as in this respect at any rate she must be accorded the same freedom of choice as her subjects. The criticisms of the 'court' are of a different order, but are equally devoid of content. The Queen has a remarkably small staff to assist her discharge her constitutional and ceremonial duties and they are noted for their unobtrusiveness and efficiency. Recently the whole royal system of administration was subjected to a radical overhaul by modern efficiency experts, a trial which the House of Commons has yet to experience. Nationals of Commonwealth countries serve on the Queen's staff and her new press secretary is an Australian.

Under the guidance of Prince Philip the monarchy far from

remaining static is constantly altering and developing.[1] His keen interest in science and British industry has connected the monarch with areas of the national life which otherwise might have been remote from her. The Queen's Awards for industry have been instituted and proved highly successful. The presentation parties for debutantes have been abolished and cocktail parties and informal luncheon parties for people of widely different backgrounds have been introduced. The dangers of becoming identified with a declining class have been avoided. Special garden parties are held from time to time for such organizations as the Women's Institutes, the Commonwealth universities and Scottish youth. Garden parties have become national rather than social events. The whole protocol that formerly surrounded royalty has been greatly simplified and informality emphasized wherever possible. The Queen attends press receptions both at home and abroad and Prince Philip gives interviews. Ceremonial is confined to official and diplomatic occasions when it is meticulously carried out. This process of gradual and judicious modernization is continuing.

Today the British monarchy is as firmly established as at any time in its long history. Maintaining its role as one of the 'dignified' parts of the constitution it has nevertheless changed with the times and brought itself up to date. The Queen's dedicated discharge of her duties constitutes both a challenge and an example to the country. The nation reveres the Queen, but the excessive adulation which threatened the monarchy in the 1950s and called forth the criticism of Lord Altrincham has declined.[2] The British monarchy seems destined to serve the nation for many years to come.

[1] 'To survive' he has stated, 'the monarchy has to change'. His outspokenness has at times been criticized, but a consort should have greater freedom of speech than the sovereign and by his utterances Prince Philip has facilitated the adaptation of the monarchy to changed conditions by projecting a new 'image' of its character.

[2] Lord Altrincham's statements on the monarchy in 1957 caused a furore. In fact his criticisms were more of the court than the Queen herself although some of his references to her were imprudent. Lord Altrincham is of course no republican but a convinced monarchist and was endeavouring to spur the monarchy on to change. Unfortunately his position was widely misunderstood. (See p. 43.)